Caro aluno, seja bem-vindo à sua plataforma do conhecimento!

A partir de agora, você tem à sua disposição uma plataforma que reúne, em um só lugar, recursos educacionais digitais que complementam os livros impressos e são desenvolvidos especialmente para auxiliar você em seus estudos. Veja como é fácil e rápido acessar os recursos deste projeto.

1 Faça a ativação dos códigos dos seus livros.

Se você NÃO tiver cadastro na plataforma:

- Para acessar os recursos digitais, você precisa estar cadastrado na plataforma educamos.sm. Em seu computador, acesse o endereço <br.educamos.sm>.
- No canto superior direito, clique em "**Primeiro acesso? Clique aqui**". Para iniciar o cadastro, insira o código indicado abaixo.
- Depois de incluir todos os códigos, clique em "**Registrar-se**" e, em seguida, preencha o formulário para concluir esta etapa.

Se você JÁ fez cadastro na plataforma:

- Em seu computador, acesse a plataforma e faça o *login* no canto superior direito.
- Em seguida, você visualizará os livros que já estão ativados em seu perfil. Clique no botão "**Adicionar livro**" e insira o código abaixo.

Este é o seu código de ativação! → **D9SHH-YCMBR-AAGYP**

I WORLD ING 1 (LA) ED 2018

2 Acesse os recursos.

Usando um computador

Acesse o endereço <br.educamos.sm> e faça o *login* no canto superior direito. Nessa página, você visualizará todos os seus livros cadastrados. Para acessar o livro desejado, basta clicar na sua capa.

Usando um dispositivo móvel

Instale o aplicativo **educamos.sm**, que está disponível gratuitamente na loja de aplicativos do dispositivo. Utilize o mesmo *login* e a mesma senha da plataforma para acessar o aplicativo.

Importante! Não se esqueça de sempre cadastrar seus livros da SM em seu perfil. Assim, você garante a visualização dos seus conteúdos, seja no computador, seja no dispositivo móvel. Em caso de dúvida, entre em contato com nosso atendimento pelo **telefone 0800 72 54876** ou pelo *e-mail* **atendimento@grupo-sm.com**.

03603

STUDENT'S BOOK
& WORKBOOK

i-WORLD | 1

MICHAEL DOWNIE • DAVID GRAY • JUAN MANUEL JIMENEZ

Know Your Book

My World sections have a cross-curricular focus and present and practice new language through *Reading, Vocabulary, Listening, Grammar,* and *Speaking* activities.

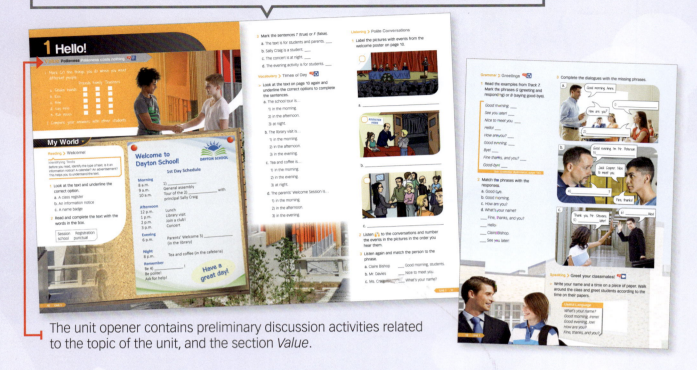

The unit opener contains preliminary discussion activities related to the topic of the unit, and the section *Value*.

Views sections focus on life skills and personalization and present and practice new language through *Listening, Vocabulary* and/or *Pronunciation, Speaking, Reading, Grammar,* and *Writing* activities.

Icons indicating digital activities, and videos links available on **educamos·sm** are found at point of use. See *Icon Key* on Teacher's Guide, page T11.

2 Know Your Book

Out and About sections have a cross-cultural focus and present and practice new language through *Reading*, *Writing*, *Listening*, *Grammar*, *Vocabulary* and *Speaking* activities.

The *Review* practices functional grammar and vocabulary presented in the unit.

A collaborative *Project* leads to a written or oral presentation using the language and topics studied every two units.

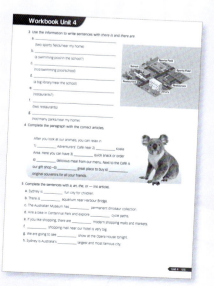

Communicative *Pairwork* activities are found at the back of the book, along with a complete *Grammar Reference* of the language covered throughout the level, and a *Workbook* for additional practice.

Enriched digital book available on educamos·sm

Know Your Book 3

Contents

Hello i-World! 6

Unit	Grammar	Vocabulary	Reading
1 Hello! p. 10	Greetings Classroom Language (1) Classroom Language (2)	Times of day Around school	An information notice A comic strip Dictionary entries
2 Friends Around the World p. 20	Possessives *My/Your* *To be* 1st and 3rd Person *To be* 2nd Person (Questions and Short Answers)	Sports Days of the week	Online profiles Online posts A schedule and an announcement
3 Global World p. 30	Simple Present *To be* 3rd Person (Questions and Short Answers) Simple Present *To be* (Plurals) Question Words	Countries and nationalities Colors	Articles Interview
4 A Great Place p. 40	*There is/There are* Articles (*a/an/the*) Directions	Places in a city Transport The beach	A website A flyer A tourist guide
5 Family Matters p. 50	*Have/Has* Demonstrative Pronouns Possessive *'s*	Family members Months Describing people	A quiz A comic strip An article
6 Here and There p. 60	Simple Present *I, You* Simple Present (3rd Person Singular) Simple Present for Routines: *We, They*, and Adverbs of Frequency	Daily routines Telling the time	Articles An interview
7 Food World p. 70	*Some/Any* *Can* for Ability Offers and Suggestions	Food Dishes Eating out	Magazine articles A web article
8 Home, Sweet Home p. 80	Present Continuous *I, You* Present Continuous (3rd Person Singular) *Can* for Requests	House chores Places in a house Furniture	A news site A book summary A web article

Listening	Speaking	Writing
Conversations	Greetings **Pronunciation:** Numbers 1–10	Dictionary entries A quiz
A video call An interview A conversation	A registration **Pronunciation:** Numbers 11–20	A web profile A survey A post An e-mail
A game show An interview A quiz	A game A quiz **Pronunciation:** The alphabet	A celebrity profile An interview A description
A conversation Tourist information Instructions	Descriptions Directions **Pronunciation:** The schwa	A website section A letter A flyer An ad
A radio program A class A conversation	A description **Pronunciation:** Word stress	A quiz A comic strip A survey
Interviews	An interview **Pronunciation:** Plurals /s/ vs /iz/	A description Interviews An article
Conversations Ordering food	Information gaps A conversation A role-play **Pronunciation:** /ʌ/ vs /uː/	A quiz
Interviews A radio ad Conversations	A project presentation A conversation Requests **Pronunciation:** /b/ vs /v/	A description Rules

Pairwork 90

Projects 94

Grammar Reference 102

Numbers, Days of the Week, Months 108

Alphabet 109

Phonetic Symbols 110

Irregular Verbs 111

Workbook 112

Hello i-World!

1 Read and complete with the words in the box.

units   skills   i-World   projects

Hi Students,

Welcome to English! We are Mike and David and we are the authors of 1) _____.

There are eight 2) _____ in i-World. Each unit has a different topic. The topic of Unit Two, for example, is friends and the topic of Unit Seven is food.

In each topic we teach four important 3) _____: reading, listening, speaking and writing. There is also vocabulary and grammar. In Unit Five you learn words for family members and in Unit Six you learn to tell the time.

You also do fun 4) _____ in i-World. In Project One, for example, you make a phrasebook and in Project Two you make a poster about your country.

Enjoy English! Enjoy i-World. Have a great year!

Mike, David and Juan

2 Listen and check.

3 Work in pairs. Look at your book and do the quiz.

DO YOU KNOW...   i-World QUIZ

1. the number of units in your book? a) nine   b) six   c) eight   d) ten
2. the topic of Unit 7?   a) school   b) food   c) sports   d) family
3. the vocabulary of Unit 5?   a) numbers   b) animals   c) colors   d) family members
4. the color of this page?   a) pink   b) blue   c) yellow   d) green

4 Work in pairs. Look at the English alphabet and say how many letters it has.

A B C D E F G H I J K L M
N O P Q R S T U V W X Y Z

5 Listen and say the letters.

6 Match the words to a color.

a. red   b. blue   c. green   d. yellow   e. white   f. black   g. orange   h. pink

7 Play Spell it! Point at a color and spell the word.

8 Listen to Holly and write the information in the calendar.

a. School starts   b. School ends   c. Vacation   d. Tests

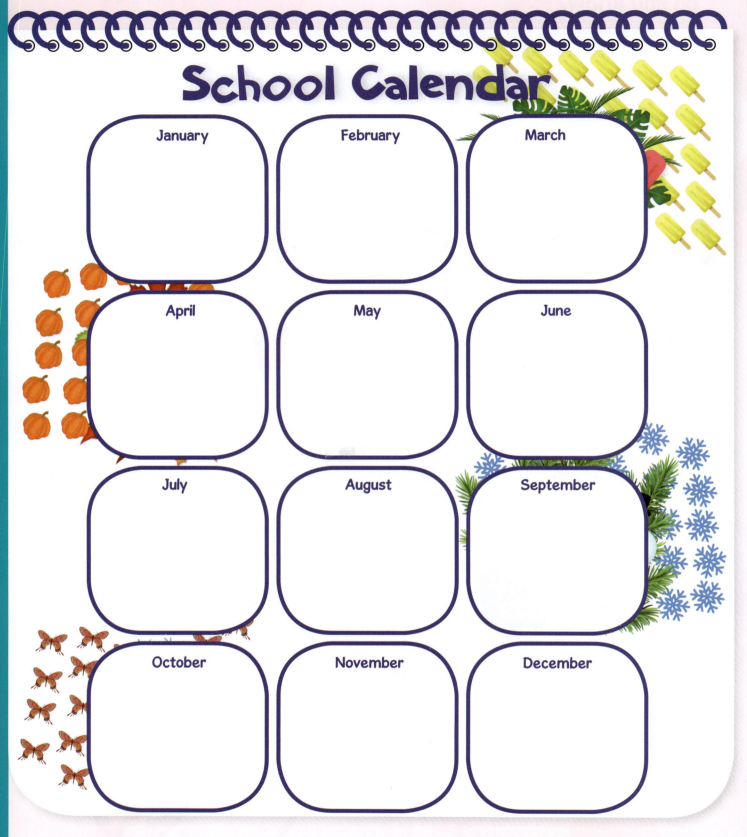

School Calendar

January	February	March
April	May	June
July	August	September
October	November	December

9 Listen and repeat.

10 Write information for your school year in the calendar.

11 Work in pairs. Compare calendars.

8   Hello!

12 Read and circle the days Sam, Pam and Tim study English.

13 Circle the days you study English at school.

Monday   Tuesday   Wednesday

Thursday   Friday

Saturday   Sunday

14 Listen and repeat.

1 Hello!

Value Politeness Politeness costs nothing

1 Mark (✓) the things you do when you meet different people.

	Friends	Family	Teachers
a. Shake hands	☐	☐	☐
b. Kiss	☐	☐	☐
c. Bow	☐	☐	☐
d. Say hello	☐	☐	☐
e. Rub noses	☐	☐	☐

2 Compare your answers with other students.

My World

Reading > Welcome!

Identifying Texts
Before you read, identify the type of text. Is it an information notice? A calendar? An advertisement? This helps you to understand the text.

1 Look at the text and underline the correct option.
   a. A class register
   b. An information notice
   c. A name badge

2 Read and complete the text with the words in the box.

| Session | Registration |
| school | punctual |

Welcome to Dayton School!

1st Day Schedule

Morning
8 a.m.   1) _____
9 a.m.   General assembly
10 a.m.   Tour of the 2) _____ with principal Sally Craig

Afternoon
12 p.m.   Lunch
1 p.m.   Library visit
2 p.m.   Join a club!
3 p.m.   Concert

Evening
6 p.m.   Parents' Welcome 3) _____ (in the library)

Night
8 p.m.   Tea and coffee (in the cafeteria)

Remember
Be 4) _____ !
Be polite!
Ask for help!

Have a great day!

10 Unit 1

3 Mark the sentences *T* (true) or *F* (false).

   a. The text is for students and parents. ___

   b. Sally Craig is a student. ___

   c. The concert is at night. ___

   d. The evening activity is for students. ___

Vocabulary > Times of Day

> Look at the text on page 10 again and underline the correct options to complete the sentences.

   a. The school tour is…

   1) in the morning.
   2) in the afternoon.
   3) at night.

   b. The library visit is…

   1) in the morning.
   2) in the afternoon.
   3) in the evening.

   c. Tea and coffee is…

   1) in the morning.
   2) in the evening.
   3) at night.

   d. The parents' Welcome Session is…

   1) in the morning.
   2) in the afternoon.
   3) in the evening.

Listening > Polite Conversations

1 Label the pictures with events from the welcome poster on page 10.

a. _____

b. _____

c. _____

2 Listen to the conversations and number the events in the pictures in the order you hear them.

3 Listen again and match the person to the phrase.

   a. Claire Bishop   ___ Good morning, students.
   b. Mr. Davies   ___ Nice to meet you.
   c. Ms. Craig   ___ What's your name?

Unit 1 11

Grammar > Greetings

1. Read the examples from *Track 7*. Mark the phrases *G* (greeting and responding) or *B* (saying good-bye).

   > Good morning. ___
   > See you later! ___
   > Nice to meet you. ___
   > Hello! ___
   > How are you? ___
   > Good evening. ___
   > Bye! ___
   > Fine thanks, and you? ___
   > Good-bye! ___
   >
   > See *Grammar Reference*, page 102.

2. Match the phrases with the responses.

   a. Good-bye.
   b. Good morning.
   c. How are you?
   d. What's your name?

   ___ Fine, thanks, and you?
   ___ Hello!
   ___ Claire Bishop.
   ___ See you later!

3. Complete the dialogues with the missing phrases.

   a.
   - Good morning, Anne.
   - 1) _____
   - How are you?
   - 2) _____

   b.
   - Good evening, I'm Mr. Peterson. 3) _____
   - Jack Cooper. Nice to meet you.
   - 4) _____?
   - Fine, thanks!

   c.
   - Thank you, Mr. Stevens. 5) _____ later!
   - 6) _____ Alex!

Speaking > Greet your classmates!

> Write your name and a time on a piece of paper. Walk around the class and greet students according to the time on their papers.

Useful Language

What's your name?
Good morning, Irene!
Good evening, Joe!
How are you?
Fine, thanks, and you?

Views

Listening > Phone Numbers

Using Context
Before you listen, look at the pictures and think about the context.

1 Work in pairs. Look at the picture and discuss the questions.

   a. Where are the people?   b. What are they doing?

2 Listen to the conversations and match the people with the activity they do.

   a. Mark and James   b. Janine and Sophia

3 Listen again and underline the correct options.

   a. Mark and James's conversation is…
      1) in the morning.   2) in the evening.   3) at night.
   b. Mark and James exchange…
      1) names.   2) phones.   3) numbers.
   c. Janine and Sophia's conversation is…
      1) in the morning   2) in the afternoon.   3) in the evening.
   d. The basketball game is at…
      1) 2 p.m.   2) 3 p.m.   3) 4 p.m.

Pronunciation > Numbers 1 – 10

1 Match the numerals to the words.

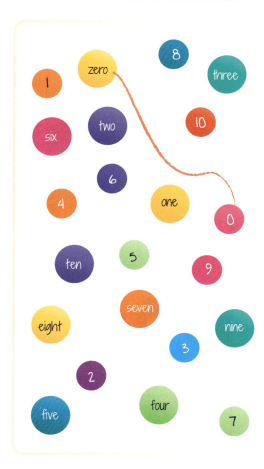

2 Listen and repeat the numbers.

3 Listen and write the phone numbers in the contact list.

Unit 1   13

Reading > Late for Class

1 Work in pairs. Look at the comic strip and underline where the people are.

   a. At home   b. At school   c. At home and at school

2 Read the comic strip and complete the Class Register.

3 Complete the sentences about the comic strip.

   a. The teacher's name is _____.
   b. The teacher is checking a _____.
   c. Robert is _____.
   d. Andrea needs to borrow a _____.

14   Unit 1

Grammar > Classroom Language (1)

1 Read the examples from the comic strip. Mark the sentences *R* (polite requests) or *I* (instructions).

May I come in? ___
Sit down. ___
Take out your books. ___
Listen for your name. ___
May I borrow a book? ___

See *Grammar Reference*, page 102.

2 Read the examples again and identify the word we use to form a polite request.

3 Complete the instructions.

| Come | Sit | Raise | Close | Open | Stand |

a. _____ up.

b. _____ the door.

c. _____ your hand.

d. _____ your book.

e. _____ down.

f. _____ in.

Unit 1   15

Out and About

Reading > **Using a Dictionary**

1 Label the types of dictionaries.

a. A bilingual dictionary

b. An English dictionary

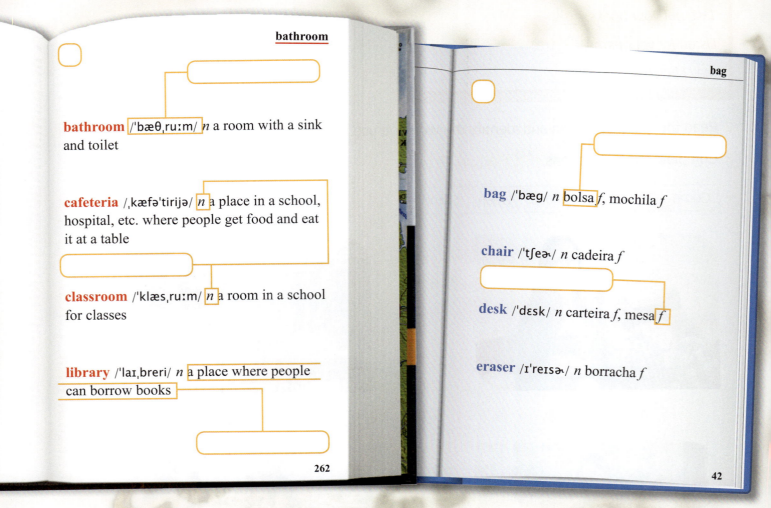

2 Read the dictionary entries and label the parts of the texts.

> translation   pronunciation   definition   gender   type of word

3 Underline the correct options.

a. The dictionaries show masculine and feminine forms with *English/Portuguese* words.

b. The dictionaries show pronunciation with *English/Portuguese* words.

c. The words on these dictionary pages are *nouns/adjectives*.

d. You borrow books from a *cafeteria/library*.

4 What types of dictionaries do you use?

a. English

b. English-Portuguese

c. Online

d. Picture

16   Unit 1

Vocabulary › Around School

1 Use the words from the dictionary pages to label the pictures.

2 Categorize the words in the table.

Objects at school	Places at school

Writing › Recording Vocabulary

1 In your notebook write two new dictionary entries for each category in the table.

2 Work in pairs. Check your entries.

Listening › Classroom Objects

1 Look at the picture and answer the questions.
   a. Where are the students?
   b. What can you see in the picture?

2 Listen and complete the online translations.

| match   underline   write |

   a. _____ emparelhar
   b. _____ escrever
   c. _____ sublinhar

3 Listen again and match the students with the items they ask about.

   a. Raquel   ___ underline
   b. Daniel   ___ match
   c. Gabriela ___ write

4 Find examples of these words in your book until this page.

Unit 1   17

Grammar > Classroom Language (2)

1 Read the extracts. Mark (✓) the sentences that ask for information.

> *What does "match" mean?* ___
>
> *How do you say* escrever *in English?* ___
>
> *Can you repeat that?* ___
>
> *I don't understand.* ___
>
> See *Grammar Reference,* page 102.

2 Match the two parts of the sentences.

a. What does…   ___ repeat that, please?

b. How do you say…   ___ *dicionário* in English?

c. Can you…   ___ don't understand.

d. Sorry, I…   ___ "notebook" mean?

3 Complete the mini-dialogues.

a. How _____ you _____ *quadro branco* in English? — Whiteboard.

b. Everyone stand up. / Stand up! — _____ _____ repeat that, please?

c. Turn to page 19. — I don't _____.

d. What _____ "notebook" _____? — It means *caderno*. — Thank you.

Writing > A Quiz

> Write five questions about the names of different things in the classroom.
>
> *How do you say* mochila *in English?*
>
> *What does "book" mean?*

Review

1 Complete the crossword.

Across →
3 A greeting at 8 a.m.
4 The answer is "Fine, thanks." The question is…
6 A greeting at 6 p.m.

Down ↓
1 A greeting at 3 p.m.
2 Hello (informal).
5 … to our school.

2 Underline the correct responses.

a. Good evening, Mrs. Harvey.
   1) See you later! 2) Good night. 3) Hello!

b. How are you?
   1) Hi! 2) Thank you. 3) Fine, and you?

c. Welcome to Dayton School.
   1) Thank you. 2) See you later! 3) And you?

d. Good-bye.
   1) Good evening. 2) See you later! 3) Welcome!

e. Good evening. I'm Mr. Smith, the principal.
   1) Bye! 2) What's your name? 3) Nice to meet you.

3 Work in pairs. Play the math game.
- Write three math problems with numbers 1 to 10.
  2 + 3 + 4 − 7
- Give the problems to your partner to answer aloud.

4 Write polite requests for the situations. Use the prompts.

window

a. _____

window

b. _____

bathroom

c. _____

5 Answer the questions.

a. How do you say *caderno* in English?
   _____

b. What does "whiteboard" mean?
   _____

c. How do you say *lápis* in English?
   _____

d. What does "underline" mean?
   _____

6 Use your notebook to make a list of polite phrases and when you use them.

2 Friends Around the World

Value Privacy Privacy protects us when we interact with the world

1 Mark (✓) what you do online.

	Yes	No
Give your real name.	☐	☐
Use a password with letters.	☐	☐
Use a password with letters and numbers.	☐	☐
Give your home address.	☐	☐
Give your phone number.	☐	☐

2 Compare in groups. Say which things are not safe to do.

HOME | FAQ | SITEMAP | CONTACT

GLOBAL FRIENDS

A great place to make friends with other teens around the world!

Join now! It's fun and safe!

What you can do

 1) _____   Post photos   Video chat   2) _____

PROFILE

Username: VickiB
Age: 14

☺ 3) _____
Place: Chicago
Sport: Basketball
Person: Pau Gasol

Hi! My name's Vicki. I'm 14. I'm from Chicago. My favorite sport is basketball and the Chicago Bulls are my favorite team. Pau Gasol is great!

Click to 4) _____ 📞

PROFILE

Username: CarlPY
Age: 15

☺ Favorites
Place: Texas
Sport: Football
Person: Selena Gomez

Hello! My name's Carl. I'm 15. I'm from Dallas, Texas. My favorite sport is football. The Dallas Cowboys are my favorite team. My favorite person is Selena Gomez. She's from Texas too.

Click to contact 📞

PROFILE

Username: PamCam
Age: 14

☺ Favorites
Place: Paris, France
Sport: Tennis
Person: Serena Williams

Hi there! My name is Pamela. I'm 14. I'm from London but my favorite place is Paris in France. It's beautiful. My favorite sport is tennis. Serena Williams is my favorite sportsperson. She's incredible. Who's your favorite?

Click to contact 📞

About Us | Members | Blog | Gallery | Newsletter | Follow Us | Support

My World

Reading > Global Friends

Using Images
Before you read, look at the images in a text (photos, icons, etc.). They help you understand the language.

1 Look at the web page on page 20 and fill in the blanks with the words in the box.

> contact   message
> favorites   games

2 Read the web page and mark the sentences *T* (true) or *F* (false).

a. Global Friends is for adults. ___

b. It is possible to post photos on Global Friends. ___

c. Profiles on Global Friends include e-mail addresses. ___

d. Profiles on Global Friends include telephone numbers. ___

3 Look at the web page again and underline the correct options to complete the sentences.

a. Vicki is from *Dallas/Chicago/London*.

b. Vicki's favorite team is the *Dallas Cowboys/Chicago Bulls/LA Lakers*.

c. Carl's favorite sport is *basketball/tennis/football*.

d. Selena Gomez is from *New York/Florida/Texas*.

e. Pamela is from *Paris/London/Texas*.

f. *Basketball/Football/Tennis* is Pamela's favorite sport.

Vocabulary > Sports

1 Label the pictures.

> basketball   tennis   swimming   baseball
> soccer   football   volleyball   athletics

_____   _____   _____   _____

_____   _____   _____   _____

2 Use your notebook to write the names of six sportspeople.

Writing > A Web Profile

> Complete the web profile for yourself.

PROFILE

Username _____   Age _____
Favorites
Place _____   Person _____
Sport _____
Hi there! My name is _____.
I'm _____. I'm from _____. My favorite sport is _____ and _____ is my favorite team. My favorite person is _____.
What's your favorite sport? Who's your favorite person?
Click to contact 📞

Listening > A Video Call

1 Listen to the start of the conversation. Decide if the boy and girl are friends.

2 Listen to the conversation and complete the chart.

	Favorite Sport	Favorite Person
Nikki		
Jack		

Unit 2   21

Grammar > Possessives *My/Your*

1 Read the extract and circle the correct options.

> *What's your favorite sport? My favorite sport is swimming.*
> See *Grammar Reference,* page 102.

a. *My/Your* refers to the speaker.
b. *My/Your* refers to the other person.

2 Underline the correct options.

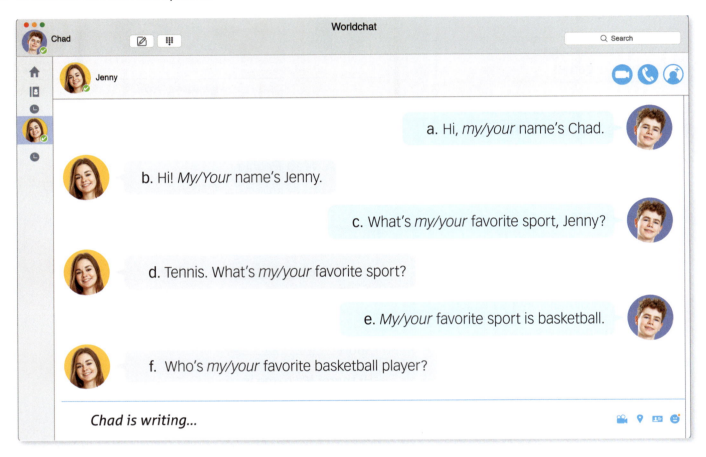

a. Hi, *my/your* name's Chad.
b. Hi! *My/Your* name's Jenny.
c. What's *my/your* favorite sport, Jenny?
d. Tennis. What's *my/your* favorite sport?
e. *My/your* favorite sport is basketball.
f. Who's *my/your* favorite basketball player?

3 Work in pairs. Ask and answer questions about favorite sports and sportspeople.

Writing > Family Poll

1 Write the questions you need to ask for a family poll on sports.

Name *What's your name?*
Favorite sport _____
Favorite sportsperson _____
Favorite team _____

2 At home, ask the questions to your family. Write the answers in your notebook.

3 Compare the information and find the most popular sports, sportspeople, and teams.

Views

Listening > Meet the Fans

Listening for Specific Information
When you listen for specific information, do not try to understand everything. Concentrate on the information you need.

1 Work in pairs. Look at the webpage and discuss the questions.
   a. What is the name of the band?
   b. What is the name of the radio station?
   c. What time is the morning program?

2 Listen to part 1 of the interview and underline the correct options.
   a. The phone number for "Meet the Fans" is 456 278 *1319/1329*.
   b. John is from *Boston/New York*.
   c. Logan is from *Boston/Miami*.
   d. Jed is from *Miami/New York*.

3 Listen to part 2. Match the sentence halves.
   a. Miguel is   ___ surfing.
   b. Logan's favorite song is   ___ from São Paulo.
   c. John's favorite song is   ___ soccer.
   d. Jed's favorite sport is   ___ "Your Eyes".
   e. Paula's favorite sport is   ___ "I am".

Pronunciation > Numbers 11 – 20

1 Write the correct number next to the word.
   a. thirteen _13_
   b. eighteen ___
   c. eleven ___
   d. fifteen ___
   e. twenty ___
   f. sixteen ___
   g. twelve ___
   h. fourteen ___
   i. seventeen ___
   j. nineteen ___

2 Listen and repeat the numbers.

3 Listen to part of the interview again and write the ages.
   a. Jed _____
   b. Logan _____
   c. John _____

Unit 2 23

Reading > Fan Posts

1 Read the posts and write the correct names in the replies.

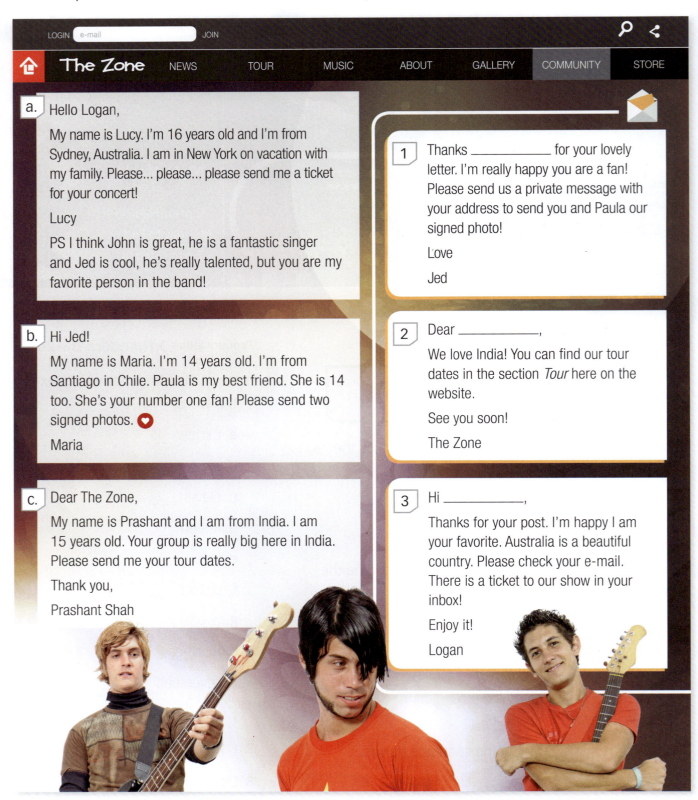

2 Read the posts again and answer the questions.
   a. How old is Lucy? _____
   b. Where is Maria from? _____
   c. Is Paula a fan of The Zone? _____
   d. What does Prashant want? _____

Grammar > *To be* 1st and 3rd Person

1 Read the extracts and underline the forms of *to be*.

> I'<u>m</u> 16 years old.
> I <u>am</u> in New York.
> John is great.
> He is a fantastic singer.
> He's really talented.
> Paula is my best friend.
> She is 14 too.
> She's your number one fan.

See *Grammar Reference,* page 102.

2 Underline the correct options to complete the sentences.
   a. **He** refers to a *boy/girl*.
   b. **She** refers to a *boy/girl*.
   c. After **I** we use *am/is*.
   d. After **he** or **she**, we use *am/is*.

3 Write the contractions.
   a. I am   I'm
   b. He is _____
   c. She is _____

4 Complete the sentences with the words in the box.

   She   He's   is   She's   He

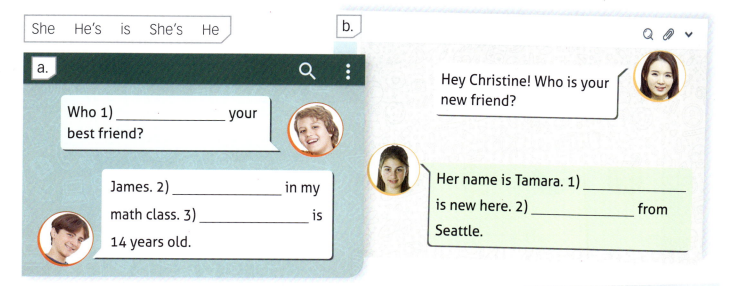

a.
Who 1) _____ your best friend?
James. 2) _____ in my math class. 3) _____ is 14 years old.

b.
Hey Christine! Who is your new friend?
Her name is Tamara. 1) _____ is new here. 2) _____ from Seattle.

Writing > A Post

> Write a post for your favorite singer or band's website. Include:
  • A greeting
  • Your name and your friend's name
  • Your ages
  • Where you're from
  • A request (a ticket, a photo, etc.) from you and your friend

Unit 2   25

Out and About

Reading > Free Time

1. Look at the texts and answer the questions.
   a. What are the types of texts?
   b. Who are the texts for?
   c. Is there a community center in your area? What activities can people do there?

2. Read the texts again. Mark the sentences T (true) or F (false).
   a. Art classes are on Monday and Saturday afternoon. ___
   b. Sculpture classes are on Tuesday and Thursday. ___
   c. Sunday is family picnic. ___
   d. Yoga class is on Monday and Friday. ___
   e. Family Movie Night is on Sunday. ___

3. Read the texts and complete the sentences.
   a. The schedule is for the _____ Community Center.
   b. Photography class offers a special _____.
   c. You need to e-mail to _____ for classes.
   d. You can _____ to ask for information.

Larkston Community Center
Schedule of Classes

	Monday	Tuesday	Wednesday	Thursday	Friday	Saturday	Sunday
Morning	Singing	Tai Chi	Yoga	Tai Chi		Singing / Singing / Ceramics	
Afternoon	Yoga	Art / Judo	Singing	Art / Judo		Modern Dance / Photography	
Evening	Modern Dance	Sculpture	Modern Dance	Sculpture	Photography		Family Movie Night

To register for classes e-mail: center@larkston.org
Information and questions call: 212.756.3691

Larkston Community Center Photography Class

Friday evenings or Saturday afternoons

*Register now and join our special trip to the Dale National Park!

Vocabulary > Days of the Week

1 Listen and write the days of the week in the correct order in your notebook.

> Thursday   Monday   Saturday   Sunday
> Wednesday   Tuesday   Friday

2 Close your book. Try to remember the days of the week in order.

3 In your notebook write your after-school and weekend schedule.

Writing > Expressing Interest

> Read the mail and complete the information.

To: center@larkston.org
From: jaselong@gmail.com
Subject: Registration

Hi!

My name is Jason Long and I am 15 years old. I am a student at Larkston High School. My favorite subject at school is art and I want to register for your art class on Thursday afternoon. I also want to register for the ceramics class on Saturday morning.

Please send me the registration forms.

Thank you,

Jason Long

Name: _____
School: _____
Favorite subject: _____
Classes: _____
Schedule: _____
_____

Listening > Registering for a Class

1 Look at the class ad on page 26 and answer the questions.

a. What is the name of the class? _____
b. What day is the class? _____
c. What is the special activity? _____

2 Listen and complete the registration form.

**Larkston Community Center
Photography Class**

Name: Jane   Last name: Flaherty

Age: 1) _____
Phone number: 2) _____
E-mail: janef@gmail.com
3) _____: Frankston High
Schedule: 4) _____ afternoon

3 Listen again and underline what the receptionist says.

a. JANE: I want to register for the photography class on Saturday afternoon.
RECEPTIONIST: Great! What's your *name/age*?

b. JANE: (440) 987-3655
RECEPTIONIST: Sorry, can you *say/repeat* that?

c. RECEPTIONIST: OK, Jane. Welcome to *photography class/Larkston*!

Grammar > *To be* 2nd Person (Questions and Short Answers)

1. Read the extracts and underline the forms of *to be*.

> *Are you at high school?*
> *Yes, I am.*
> *Are you from Larkston?*
> *No, I'm not.*
>
> See *Grammar Reference,* page 102.

2. Underline the correct forms.
   a. The form for a question is *you are/are you.*
   b. To answer "yes," we say "yes, *I am/I'm.*"
   c. To answer "no," we say "no, *I'm/I'm not.*"

3. Complete the conversations.
   a. – _____ _____ from here?
      – Yes, _____ _____.
   b. – Are you from the US?
      – No, _____ _____.

4. Use the prompts to write the conversations.

   Conversation 1
   BRIAN: 1) _____ (How old / you?)
   HILLARY: 2) _____ (I / 17)
   BRIAN: 3) _____ (you a student?)
   HILLARY: 4) _____ (No / not)

   Conversation 2
   GLEN: 5) _____ (you / Mexico?)
   FABIOLA: 6) _____ (Yes / am)
   GLEN: 7) _____ (How old / you?)
   FABIOLA: 8) _____ (I / 15)

5. Work in pairs. Practice the conversations with information about you.

Speaking > Registering for a Club

> Work in pairs. Register for a club.
> Student A: Turn to page 90.
> Student B: Turn to page 92.

Review

1 Circle the names of eight sports.

B	A	S	E	B	A	L	L	T	V
A	S	W	I	M	M	I	N	G	O
S	O	Q	W	E	R	T	Y	T	L
K	C	U	I	O	P	A	S	E	L
E	C	F	D	G	H	J	K	N	E
T	E	L	Z	X	C	V	B	N	Y
B	R	I	V	C	J	T	V	I	B
A	T	H	L	E	T	I	C	S	A
L	S	F	O	O	T	B	A	L	L
L	R	J	J	T	R	A	V	R	L

2 Unscramble the questions and answers.

a. your / What's / name / ?
_____

b. name's / Juliana / My / .
_____

c. What's / sport / favorite / your / ?
_____

d. sport / is / My / volleyball / favorite / .
_____

e. sportsperson / favorite / your / Who's / ?
_____

f. favorite / My / Ronda Rousey / is / sportsperson / .
_____

3 Complete the conversation.

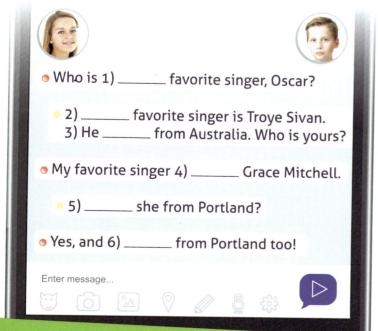

- Who is 1) _____ favorite singer, Oscar?

  - 2) _____ favorite singer is Troye Sivan.
    3) He _____ from Australia. Who is yours?

- My favorite singer 4) _____ Grace Mitchell.

  - 5) _____ she from Portland?

- Yes, and 6) _____ from Portland too!

Enter message...

4 What's your favorite singer or band?
> Write about them in your notebook.

5 Write the names and ages of four people in this unit.

a. <u>VickiB is fourteen years old.</u>

b. _____

c. _____

d. _____

e. _____

6 Write complete answers to the questions.

a. Are you from Larkston?
_____

b. Are you 15?
_____

c. Are you a student?
_____

d. Are you in the photography class?
_____

Unit 2   29

3 Global World

Value Respecting differences Respecting differences is the basis for harmony

1 Work in pairs. Discuss the questions.
   a. What's your favorite city in your country?
   b. What's your favorite festival or holiday?
   c. What's your favorite type of food?

2 Work in groups. Check if your answers are similar or different.

The Melting Pot

The United States of America is a melting pot of different cultures. People are originally from countries all around the world. For example, the family of Barack Obama, the first African-American President of the US, is originally from Kenya, Ireland, and England.

Many famous actors and singers are not originally from the US either. Here are some well-known celebrities who come from different countries. Do you know who they are and where they are from?

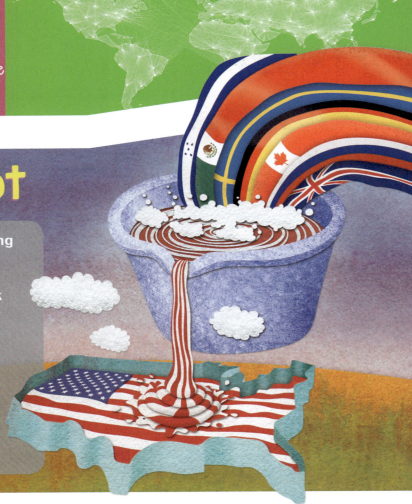

My World

Reading > Where are they from?

Using Pictures
Before you read, look at the pictures of the text. Pictures help you to understand what the text is about.

1 Look at the cartoon and mark (✓) what you think the article is about.

   a. Food ___   b. Travel ___   c. The US ___

2 Read the article and choose the best title.
   a. Celebrities Living Around the World
   b. Non-American Celebrities
   c. Americans Famous In Different Countries

3 Write the countries the people have family connections to beside the names.

   a. Barack Obama _____
   b. Liam Hemsworth _____
   c. Drake _____
   d. Rihanna _____
   e. Jordana Brewster _____

4 Answer the questions.
   a. Why is the US a melting pot?
   b. Why is Liam Hemsworth famous?
   c. What do people often say about Drake?
   d. Where is Barbados?
   e. Who is Jordana Brewster?

Are they American? Think again!

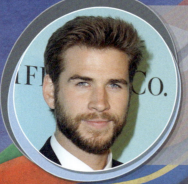

Liam Hemsworth

He is famous for his role in *The Hunger Games* movies. Many fans think he is from the US but in fact he is from Australia.

Jordana Brewster

Jordana is a famous Hollywood actress but she isn't from the US. She is from Panama. Her mother is from Brazil and her father is American.

Where is your favorite celebrity from? Are you sure?

Drake

People say that Drake is a typical American success story, but he isn't from the US at all! He is from Toronto, in Canada.

Rihanna

Rihanna isn't American? Sorry, she isn't! She's from Barbados, in the Caribbean. Her father is part Irish.

Writing > An International Celebrity Profile

1 Read the celebrity profile and complete the information about Mila Kunis.

Celebrity Profile

Birth Name: Milena Markovna Kunis
Profession: Actress
Nationality: American
Birth Date: August 14, 1983
Birth Place: Kiev, Ukraine
Claim to Fame: Lily, in the movie *Black Swan* (2010)

Mila Kunis is an _____ actress but she is originally from _____. Her birthday is on _____. Mila is famous for her role as Lily in the movie _____.

2 Create a celebrity profile about someone famous in your country.

Listening > Celebrity Quiz

1 Listen to the show and underline the theme.
   a. Celebrity names   c. Celebrity professions
   b. Celebrity nationalities d. Celebrity hobbies

2 Listen again and write the nationalities of the people.
   a. Maria _____
   b. Andy _____
   c. Rita Ora _____
   d. Ryan Reynolds _____

Vocabulary > Countries and Nationalities

> Match the countries with the nationalities.

   a. Brazil   American ___
   b. Canada   Brazilian ___
   c. France   British ___
   d. India   Italian ___
   e. Italy   Mexican ___
   f. Mexico   Spanish ___
   g. Spain   Canadian ___
   h. UK   French ___
   i. USA   Indian ___

Unit 3   31

Grammar > Simple Present *To be* 3rd Person (Questions and Short Answers)

1 Read the extracts and underline the forms of *to be*.

> *Is Ryan Reynolds from New York?*
> *No, he isn't.*
> *He's from Canada.*
>
> *Where is Rihanna from?*
> *She's from Barbados.*

See *Grammar Reference*, page 103.

2 Complete the sentences with the correct form of *to be*.

a. In affirmative answers, use _____ for *he* or *she*.

b. To form the negative of *is* use _____.

c. In questions, use _____ before the subject.

3 Match the questions with their answers.

a. Where is Rita Ora from? ___ No, he isn't.

b. Is he from Australia? ___ Yes, my dad's family is Indian.

c. Is your family from India? ___ She's from the UK.

4 Use the names to write questions.

a. (Liam Hemsworth) _____ He's from Australia.

b. (Rihanna) _____ No, she isn't. She's from Barbados.

c. (Jordana Brewster) _____ She's from Panama.

d. (Drake) _____ Yes, he is.

Speaking > Guess Who

1 Write the name of a famous person for each category.

singer	
actor	
sportsperson	

2 Work in groups. Take turns guessing the names. Score one point for each correct answer.

> **Useful Language**
> *Is it a man or a woman?*
> *Is he from...?*
> *Is she a...?*

Unit 3

Views

Listening > Multifest

Listening for Topics
The first time you listen, listen for the general topics the speakers discuss. This information will help you to understand the context.

1 Listen and number the topics in the order you hear them.

___ The website

___ The name of the festival

___ Countries represented at the festival

___ Food at the festival

2 Listen again and underline the correct answers.

   a. Multifest means *multiethnic/multicultural* festival.
   b. There are groups from Japan, Russia, India, and *Brussels/Brazil*.
   c. Simosihle means beautiful *people/music*.
   d. There is food from *Mexico/India*.
   e. The website is *www.multifest.com/ www.multifest.org*.
   f. Multifest is *this/next* Saturday and Sunday.

3 Work in groups. Discuss the questions.

   a. What festivals occur in your town or city?
   b. What activities can you do there?

Pronunciation > The Alphabet

1 Write the letters in the English alphabet.
   _____
   _____

2 Listen to check and repeat.

3 Listen again and group the letters according to the pronunciation of the vowel sound.

   /eɪ/ A, ___, J, ___
   /iː/ B, ___, ___, E, ___, ___, ___, ___, Z
   /e/   F, ___, ___, ___, S, ___
   /aɪ/ I, ___
   /əʊ/ O
   /uː/ Q, ___, W
   /ɑː/ R

Unit 3 33

Reading > Festival News

1 Look at the interview and mark (✓) the topics you will find.

___ The meaning of the name of the group ___ The costumes the group wears

___ The number of dancers in the group ___ The instruments the group plays

___ Where the group is from ___ The group's salary

___ Traditional food from the group's country ___ The cost of tickets for their show

2 Read the article to check.

Festival News

In the Spotlight: An Interview with Malungo

FESTIVAL NEWS: Thanks for the interview, Malungo. Please tell us about your name. Where does it come from?

MALUNGO: It's an African word. It means "friend."

FN: What do you do?

M: We're a traditional dance group.

FN: Are you all from Brazil?

M: Yes, we are. We're from Bahia.

FN: How many dancers are in your group?

M: In total, we're a group of eighteen dancers and musicians.

FN: Are you professional dancers?

M: No. We aren't professional dancers but we're all very serious about our project.

FN: What about your wardrobe? Are your clothes special?

M: Yes, they are. They help us move freely.

FN: They're beautiful too. I also like your musical instruments. Are they modern?

M: No, they aren't. The berimbau, for example, is the instrument used in Capoeira. Capoeira is a traditional dance in Brazil.

3 Answer the questions.

a. What does Malungo mean?

_____

b. What place is the group from?

_____

c. How many people are there in the group?

_____

d. Are the members of the group only dancers?

_____

e. Are their instruments traditional?

_____

4. Write the names of traditional songs and instruments from your community.

a. _____

b. _____

c. _____

d. _____

> Work in groups. Share your answers.

34 Unit 3

Grammar > Simple Present *To be* (Plurals)

1 Read the extracts. Label them *Q* (question), *A* (affirmative answer), or *N* (negative answer).

> *We're a traditional dance group.* ___
>
> *Are you from Brazil?* ___
>
> *Yes, we are. We're from Bahia.* ___
>
> *Are you professional dancers?* ___
>
> *We aren't professional.* ___
>
> *Are your clothes special?* ___
>
> *Yes, they are.* ___
>
> *Are they modern?* ___
>
> *They're beautiful too.* ___
>
> *No, they aren't.* ___
>
> See *Grammar Reference,* page 103.

2 Mark the rules *T* (true) or *F* (false).

a. With *we, you,* and *they* use *is*. ___

b. To form the negative of *are* use *aren't*. ___

c. To form questions use *are* before *we, you,* or *they*. ___

3 Use the prompts to complete another interview from the magazine.

Peggy Blaxall meets Viva Flamenco

PB: Thanks for your time, Viva Flamenco. I know you have a new project with Tablao.
 1) _____ (dancers too?)
VF: No, they're a flamenco band. They're Spanish.
PB: Are their instruments traditional?
VF: Not really, 2) _____ (traditional and modern)
PB: Are the guitars electric?
VF: Haha, no! 3) _____ (acoustic guitars) but they have a keyboard. Some of the musicians dance with us too.
PB: Really? 4) _____ (professional dancers too?)
VF: No, 5) _____ (professional) but they're very good dancers!
PB: I can't wait to see you tomorrow in Multifest. Good luck with your project!

Writing > An Interview

> Work in groups of four. Form two pairs.

Pair A: Read the information about your group and answer the reporter's questions.

- Group name: Jazz Beats
- From: US
- Level: professionals, not amateurs
- Instruments: guitar, bass guitar, drums

Pair B: You are reporters. Ask questions to find this information.

- Group name and where they are from
- Professional or amateur
- Their instruments

Now, work in a different pair. Write the interview.

Out and About

Reading > Colors

1 Look at the flags and answer.
   a. Where do you think they are from?
   b. What do you think the colors mean?

The Importance of Colors

Red, white, and blue are very popular colors in national flags. Many countries, like the USA, Australia, Chile, France, Paraguay, and the UK, use all three of these colors. Other common colors in flags are yellow, green, and black. Many countries in Latin America, such as Uruguay, Colombia, Brazil, and Venezuela, have yellow in their flags. Orange, brown, gray, and purple are unusual in flags and no country in the world has a pink flag!

What do the colors mean? Colors have different meanings in different countries. In China, for example, red means good luck, but in Nigeria it means bad luck. Green, in Japan, is the color of love, but in Malaysia it represents danger. In South Korea, purple is the color of love, but in Brazil it is a sad color. For people in Australia, white is a happy color, but in some Asian countries like China and Korea, white represents death.

There are many expressions with color words in English. For example, "to see red" means to become angry, and if you are "feeling blue" it means you feel sad. A person who is "green" is not experienced. What do these colors mean in your language?

2 Read the article and mark the sentences *T* (true) or *F* (false).

   a. The national flag of Paraguay has two colors. ___
   b. Green is not a common color for flags. ___
   c. The flags of Brazil and Venezuela use yellow. ___
   d. Orange is a common color for flags. ___
   e. No national flag uses pink. ___

3 Complete the chart with information from the article.

Color	Country / Region	Meaning
red		good luck
green	Japan	
purple	Brazil	
white		happy

4 Answer the questions.
   a. What expressions in your language use colors?
   b. What do different colors mean in your culture?

Vocabulary > Colors

1 Look at the flags and number the descriptions.

a. The German flag is black, red, and yellow. ___

b. The Irish flag is green, white, and orange. ___

c. The Swedish flag is blue and yellow. ___

d. The Turkish flag is red and white. ___

2 Describe the colors of the flags.

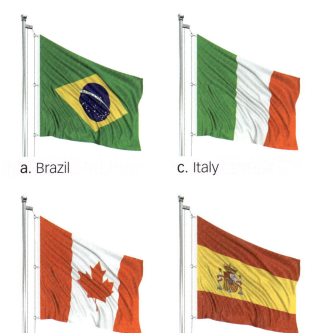

a. Brazil   c. Italy

b. Canada   d. Spain

a. _____
b. _____
c. _____
d. _____

Writing > Flag Description

1 Read the description and underline what each color means.

> The Italian flag is green, white, and red. The color green represents hope, white, faith and red, charity. The green stripe is always near the flagpole.

2 Choose a country and investigate what the colors of its flag mean.

> Write the description of the flag in your notebook.

Listening > A Country Quiz

1 Work in pairs. Say what you know about these countries.

France

United States of America

2 Listen and answer the questions.

a. What is today's quiz about?
_____

b. How many members does each team have?
_____

c. Which team spells Rushmore correctly?
_____

3 Listen again and write the points for each team.

Blue team: ___ points   Red team: ___ points

Unit 3 37

Grammar > Question Words

1 Read the extracts and underline the question words.

> *What's the capital of the US?* *Who is the father of American independence?*
> *Where is Mount Rushmore?* *How do you spell Rushmore?*
>
> See *Grammar Reference*, page 103.

2 Complete the descriptions with question words.

a. Use _____ to ask about location.

b. Use _____ to ask about a person.

c. Use _____ to ask the way to do something.

d. Use _____ to ask for information.

3 Look at the pictures. Use the prompts to write the questions for the answers.

a.
(man)
_____
He's Justin Timberlake.

b.
(Spanish)
_____
It's red and yellow.

c.
(Rio de Janeiro)
_____
It's in Brazil.

d.
(China)
_____
It's Beijing.

e.
(Brussels)
_____
B-R-U-S-S-E-L-S

Speaking > A Country Quiz

1 Work in groups. Write six questions for a country quiz.

What's the capital of Portugal?
How do you spell country?

2 Work with another group. Ask and answer your questions.

Useful Language

What color is Colombia's flag?
It's yellow, blue, and red.
Correct, you earn one point!

38 Unit 3

Review

1 Write the countries beside the nationalities.

   a. American _____
   b. French _____
   c. Indian _____
   d. Mexican _____
   e. British _____

2 Complete the conversation with the correct forms of *to be*.

Dad

- Glad you have new friends!
- Yeah! They _____ really nice.
- Where _____ they from?
- Danielle _____ from Canada.
- _____ she from Quebec?
- Hmm, I'_____ not sure.
- What about the other girl?
- She'_____ American. Her name _____ Joanna.
- Nice! Well, have a nice flight, honey. See you at the airport.
- OK, dad. I love you.

3 Unscramble the questions.

   a. the / Tower / is / where / Eiffel / ?
   _____
   b. spell / do / how / you / ? / Ukraine
   _____
   c. is / the / ? / capital / what / Argentina / of
   _____
   d. the / ? / color / is / flag / what / Mexican
   _____
   e. ? / teacher / is / who / your / English
   _____

4 Read the article and write four questions about Gaby and Akachi.

Friends from Other Countries

Gaby is from Spain. She has a lot of friends at school. She also has friends in other countries.

Gaby's best friend is Akachi. He is from South Africa. Akachi is very different from Gaby. Gaby is from a small town but Akachi is from a big city, he is from Johannesburg. His favorite soccer team is Manchester United. Gaby's favorite team is Real Madrid. But Gaby and Akachi are similar too. They are the same age. They are both 15. They are students and they are both fans of horror movies!

Gaby and Akachi

> Work in pairs. Ask and answer your questions.

Unit 3   39

4 A Great Place

Value Civic Pride Civic pride is about appreciating your community

1 In order of importance, number what makes your hometown special.
 - [ ] People
 - [ ] Location
 - [ ] Food
 - [ ] History
 - [ ] Facilities
 - [ ] Festivals

2 Compare your ranking in groups. Name three features you like about your hometown.

mysydney.au

| Getting Around (read more) | Libraries (read more) | Art and Culture (read more) | Facilities (read more) | Places to Go (read more) |

a.

Parks

Sydney has more than 400 parks, including Hyde Park and Paddington Gardens. Most parks have cafés and children's playgrounds, and in some parks there are sports fields and barbecue areas.

Swimming Pools

People in Sydney love water and the city has five aquatic centers. Each center has an Olympic swimming pool that is open all year.

c.

Cycling

Cycling is a popular way to get around in Sydney. There is a 200 km bike network in the city.

b.

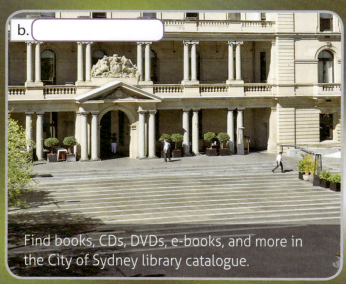

Find books, CDs, DVDs, e-books, and more in the City of Sydney library catalogue.

d.

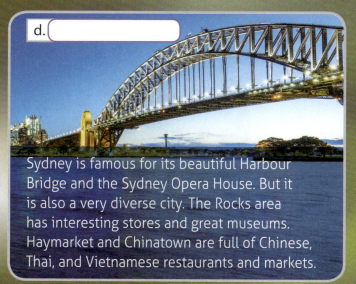

Sydney is famous for its beautiful Harbour Bridge and the Sydney Opera House. But it is also a very diverse city. The Rocks area has interesting stores and great museums. Haymarket and Chinatown are full of Chinese, Thai, and Vietnamese restaurants and markets.

My World

Reading > Sydney

> **Browsing a New Website**
> When you go on a new website, look at the menu bar. Think about the kind of information each section will contain.

1 Answer the questions.
   a. Where is Sydney?
   b. What famous places are there in Sydney?

2 Read the extracts and label the sections of the website.

3 Rewrite the sentences with the correct information.
   a. Sydney has 200 parks.
   _____
   _____

   b. The aquatic centers close in the winter.
   _____
   _____

   c. There is a 500 km cycle network in Sydney.
   _____
   _____

   d. The City of Sydney library only has books.
   _____
   _____

   e. The Rocks area has Thai and Vietnamese restaurants.
   _____
   _____

The city has lots of places to enjoy live music and drama, from the incredible Sydney Opera House to small theaters and friendly concert halls.

Vocabulary > Places in a City

> Circle the words in the website. Then match them with the definitions.
   a. market   d. library
   b. store   e. swimming pool
   c. sports field   f. playground

   ___ a place with play equipment for children
   ___ a public place to buy food, clothes, etc.
   ___ a building where you can borrow books
   ___ a building where people buy things
   ___ a place where you can play soccer, baseball, etc.
   ___ a place where you can swim

Writing > A Website Section

1 Make a list of sections to include in a website for your area.

2 Choose a section for the website and write it.

> **Useful Language**
> *The city has many interesting museums.*
> *This area is famous for its stores.*
> *Walking is a good way to move around the area.*

Listening > Choosing Places

1 Listen and underline the correct options.
   a. They are choosing places to visit in *Australia/Austria*.
   b. Johnny wants to see *emus/kangaroos*.
   c. Palm Beach is near *Canberra/Sydney*.
   d. You can *fish/swim* in Palm Beach.
   e. Johnny wants to buy local *food/music*.

2 Mark if you can find the items in Canberra (C) or Palm Beach (P).
   a. picnic ___   d. market ___
   b. beach ___   e. restaurants ___
   c. music ___   f. kangaroos ___

3 Work in pairs. Say which place you want to visit and why.

Unit 4 41

Grammar > There is/There are

1 Look at the extracts and label the sentences.

> A = affirmative   N = negative   I = interrogative

There is a lake. ___

There aren't beaches in Canberra. ___

Is there a fishing area? ___

Yes, there is. ___

Are there kangaroos? ___

No, there aren't. ___

See *Grammar Reference*, page 103.

2 Mark the sentences *T* (true) or *F* (false).

a. We use *there is* and *there are* to talk about things that exist. ___

b. We use *there is* and *there isn't* for plural sentences. ___

c. We use *there are* and *there aren't* for singular sentences. ___

d. We ask questions with *is there* and *are there*. ___

> Correct the false statements to make them true.

a. _____

b. _____

3 Complete the postcard with the correct forms of *there is/there are*.

Hi Emilio,

I'm really having fun in Melbourne. (1) _____ many beautiful beaches and the people are really nice. (2) _____ kangaroos jumping down the street, but they have some in the zoo. (3) _____ really cool street art around every corner — I love it here! The cafés and restaurants are incredible, but (4) _____ Mexican food. I miss that! (5) _____ so many things I want to show you. I promise to take a lot of pictures!

Miss you,
Betty

4 Use the prompts to write questions to ask Betty.

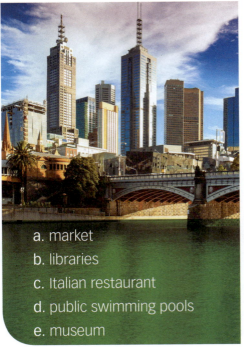

a. market
b. libraries
c. Italian restaurant
d. public swimming pools
e. museum

a. _Is there a market near your hotel?_

b. _____
_____

c. _____
_____

d. _____
_____

e. _____
_____

Writing > Tourist Attractions

1 Use your notebook to make a list of attractions in a city or town you like.

2 Write a letter to a friend about the attractions in your place.

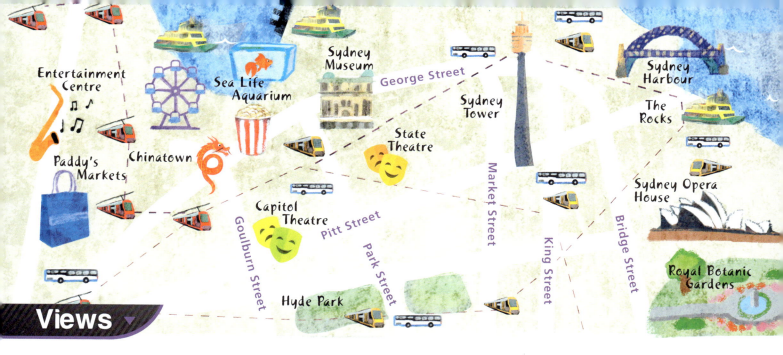

Listening > City Attractions

Listening for Place Names
When you look at a map, ask other people how place names are pronounced. This makes it easier to recognize the names when you hear them.

1 Look at the map. Mark (✗) places where you can do these activities.
- learn about aquatic life
- see unusual plants
- watch a play
- listen to a concert
- go shopping
- eat Chinese food

2 Listen and circle the attractions the hotel receptionist mentions.

3 Listen again and complete the visitors' notes.

```
Sea Life Aquarium - Open 9:30 - _____
The Rocks - Good for _____
Transport: Train station near the _____
The Opera House - Music, theater, movies and
a _____
Transport: Bus every _____ minutes
```

Pronunciation > The Schwa

1 Listen to the pronunciation of the underlined sounds (the schwa).
We'd like s<u>o</u>me inform<u>a</u>ti<u>o</u>n.
Here's <u>a</u> city <u>a</u>ttracti<u>o</u>ns map.

2 Listen again and say the sentences.

3 Listen and underline the schwa sounds in these sentences.
a. The Rocks has interesting stores.
b. The station is near the park.
c. It opens at nine.
d. They have music and theater.

Vocabulary > Transport

> Read the definitions and write the means of transportation.

| bus | ferry | subway |
| bicycle | train | taxi |

a. It has 2 wheels: _____.
b. A boat to carry people and objects for a short distance: _____.
c. Underground trains in a city: _____.
d. A car that takes passengers to a place for money: _____.
e. A large vehicle that usually has a specific route: _____.
f. A connected group of railroad cars: _____.

Unit 4   43

Speaking > **A Tourist Attraction**

1 Complete the information for a tourist attraction you like.

Opening times _____   Name of the attraction _____

How to get there _____   What you can do there _____

2 Work in pairs. Describe your attraction.

Reading > **Wild Life Sydney Zoo**

1 Look at the flyer and mark the information that appears.

   a. The location of Wild Life Sydney Zoo ____

   b. How to get to the zoo ____

   c. The price of a ticket to the zoo ____

Wild Life Sydney Zoo

Enjoy an animal adventure in the middle of the city

Come and see us!

We are on Darling Harbour, right next to Sea Life Sydney Aquarium. Getting here is easy.

Ferries to Darling Harbour leave from Circular Quay every half an hour.

We are a ten-minute walk from George Street down Market Street or King Street.

Trains stop at Town Hall Station every fifteen minutes.

Buses are very frequent. The Sydney Explorer Bus stops at the Aquarium and the City Zoo.

There are taxis everywhere in Sydney. Stop a taxi in the street or call 131008. Ask the taxi to stop at Lime Street.

For a full schedule, please check timetables on Transport Info: 131500 or https://transportnsw.info/#.

2 Answer the questions.

   a. Where do you take the ferry to Darling Harbour? _____

   b. How do you get to the zoo from George Street? _____

   c. What train station do visitors to the zoo use? _____

   d. Where does the Sydney Explorer Bus stop? _____

   e. What number do you call if you need a taxi? _____

44   Unit 4

Grammar > Articles (a/an/the)

1 Look at the extracts and match the sentences halves.

> *There are taxis everywhere in Sydney.*
> *Stop a taxi in the street or call 131008.*
> *Ask the taxi to stop at Lime Street.*
>
> See *Grammar Reference,* page 104.

a. The word *taxis* refers to ___ a specific taxi
b. The words *a taxi* refer to ___ a taxi in general (not specific)
c. The words *the taxi* refer to ___ taxis in general (plural)

2 Complete the rules.

| a   an (x2)   the   don't |

a. When we refer to a specific thing, we use _____.
b. When we refer to things in general, we _____ use an article.
c. We use _____ or _____ for non-specific singular nouns.
d. We use _____ when the noun starts with a vowel sound.

3 Underline the correct articles.

What is Wild Life Sydney Zoo?

Wild Life Sydney Zoo is *a / an* amazing attraction for the whole family. We have *the / –* koalas and kangaroos as well as *a / –* fantastic crocodile enclosure. Visitors can go into *– / the* Koala Area and take *– / the* photographs with these beautiful animals. Of course, you can't go into *a / the* crocodile enclosure! Apart from crocodiles, the enclosure is also full of *– / the* dangerous snakes and scorpions!

Writing > A Flyer for a Local Attraction

> Work in pairs. You are going to write a short flyer for an attraction in your town.
> - Choose the attraction.
> - Note down information for the following sections:
>
>   Name of the attraction
>   _____
>   _____
>
>   What visitors can do there
>   _____
>   _____
>
>   How to get there
>   _____
>   _____
>
> - Write the flyer.

Out and About

Reading › Bondi Beach

1 Work in pairs. Look at the picture and say why this place is popular.

Bondi Beach is only 7 km from the center of Sydney. It is very popular with tourists and residents. It is famous all over the world for its great surfing and scuba diving. The life under the sea is amazing!

For Surfers
There are changing rooms and showers for surfers in the historic Bondi Surf Pavilion. From there, tunnels go under Queen Elizabeth Drive to the beach. You can rent surfboards and wet suits on the beach. To learn to surf, go to one of the surf schools. Let's Go Surfing is a popular school.

To Eat
There are kiosks on the beach, and the Pavilion has a café. There are also good cafés and restaurants in the streets behind the Pavilion.

Shopping
Don't miss the Bondi Beach market, every Sunday 9 a.m. to 3 p.m. The market is beside Bondi Beach Public School. You can find cool beach fashions here.

2 Skim the guide above and number the topics in the order they are mentioned.

   a. Information about Bondi Beach market ___
   b. Why Bondi Beach is famous ___
   c. Places to eat and drink ___
   d. Facilities for surfers ___

3 Scan the guide and complete the information.

The distance from the center of Sydney to Bondi Beach: _____

Where you can change your clothes: _____

The name of a popular surf school: _____

Where to eat: _____

Opening times of Bondi Beach market: _____

46 Unit 4

Vocabulary > The Beach

> Label the elements in the picture.

a. changing room
b. scuba diving
c. shower
d. surfboard
e. surfing
f. wet suit

Listening > Asking for Directions

1 Listen and write where the visitors want to go.

a. _____
b. _____
c. _____

2 Listen again and underline the correct options.
   a. Turn *left/right* at the entrance on Campbell Parade. Go straight *three/five* blocks and turn left. Continue walking to find the beach.
   b. From Bondi Pavilion, turn right at the *car park/entrance*. Go straight and turn right on the corner. The entrance is in *the middle/on the right*.
   c. From the car park, go *straight/past* and go *straight/past* Bondi Park. Cross the street.

Writing > An Ad

> Write an ad for a local store. Include:
- Name of business
- What you sell
- Your specialty
- Your location
- Optional: special offer

Unit 4   47

Grammar > Directions

1 Read the extracts and underline the correct option to complete the rules.

> Go straight. Turn left.
> Turn right. Go past Bondi Park.
>
> See *Grammar Reference*, page 104.

a. To give directions, we use the infinitive *with/ without* to.

b. We *use/don't use* personal pronouns to give directions.

2 Follow the directions on the map and write the places.

a. Go straight two blocks and turn left. It's on the right: _____

b. Go straight one block, turn right and go past the library. It's on the left: _____

c. Go past the library and turn right. Go straight two blocks. It's on your left: _____

3 Mark (✗) a starting point in the map and complete the dialogues.

a.
VISITOR: Hello, can you help me?
LOCAL: Of course.
VISITOR: How do I get to Easy Records?
LOCAL: _____ and _____.
VISITOR: Thanks!
LOCAL: No problem.

b.
VISITOR: Hello, _____?
LOCAL: _____.
VISITOR: _____ the library?
LOCAL: _____.
VISITOR: Thank you!
LOCAL: _____
_____.

Speaking > Directions

1 Work in pairs. Draw a simple map of your school area and mark six places to get to.

2 Ask and give directions to the places.

48 Unit 4

Review

1 Work in pairs. Look at the map and say what there is in Newville.

> clothes stores   library   sports field
> restaurant   parks   swimming pool
> hotel   cafés   museum   beaches

There are three clothes stores.
There aren't any museums.

2 Complete the brochure with *a, an, the,* or no article.

Newville is (1) _____ wonderful place to live. The town has (2) _____ swimming pool, (3) _____ sports field, and (4) _____ two beautiful parks. There is also (5) _____ good library. (6) _____ main shopping area is downtown. There is (7) _____ big hotel in the town center. (8) _____ hotel has (9) _____ very good Italian restaurant.

3 Read the article and say what special events the Moomba Festival has.

The Moomba Festival

The Moomba Festival happens every year in Melbourne, Australia. It is a free community festival and more than a million people attend.

The Moomba has events for the whole family, including spectacular fireworks, parades, and live music. One unusual event is the Birdman Rally, when people use homemade flying devices to jump from the banks of the Yarra River. The winner is the person who flies the longest distance.

People in Melbourne are very proud of their city and they love to welcome visitors to their festival.

> Answer the questions in your notebook.
> a. How do people in Melbourne feel about their city?
> b. What makes you feel proud of your hometown?

Unit 4   49

5 Family Matters

Value Identity Our family is the basis of our identity and our values

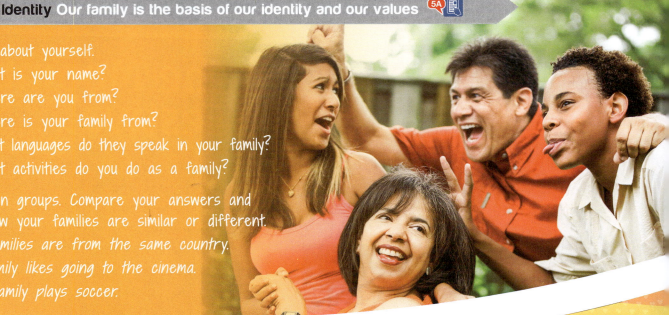

1 Think about yourself.
   a. What is your name?
   b. Where are you from?
   c. Where is your family from?
   d. What languages do they speak in your family?
   e. What activities do you do as a family?

2 Work in groups. Compare your answers and say how your families are similar or different.
   Our families are from the same country.
   My family likes going to the cinema.
   Your family plays soccer.

Celebrity Family Mastermind Quiz

How well do you know your celebrities? Does your favorite celebrity have a famous mom or dad or perhaps a secret cousin? How many brothers and sisters do they have? Take our quiz to find out!

1 How many brothers does Leonardo DiCaprio have?
   a) Two   b) None, he has a sister.   c) None, he is an only child.
2 What job does Willow and Jaden Smith's famous father have?
   a) An actor   b) An actor and musician   c) A musician
3 Which of the Williams sisters has more tennis trophies?
   a) Serena   b) Venus   c) Yetunde
4 Are Hilary Clinton and Angelina Jolie related?
   a) Yes, they are sisters. b) Yes, they are cousins. c) No, they are not related.
5 What is the name of Victoria and David Beckham's first son?
   a) Romeo   b) Brooklyn   c) Cruz
6 How many children does Salma Hayek have?
   a) She has one daughter.   b) She has one son.   c) None
7 Who is Lily-Rose Depp's mother?
   a) Kate Moss   b) Vanessa Paradis   c) Winona Ryder
8 Which of these people has a famous grandmother?
   a) Prince Harry b) Zayn Malik   c) Felicity Jones

Now check your answers. Are you a **Celebrity Mastermind?**

Key

0 - 3: You are not interested in celebrities!

4 - 6: Mmm... not bad but you are not celebrity-obsessed.

7-8: Wow! You are a Celebrity Mastermind!

Answers
1 Leonardo is an only child.
2 Their father, Will Smith, is an actor and musician.
3 Serena has more trophies.
4 They are distant cousins.
5 Their first son's name is Brooklyn. Romeo is their second son and Cruz is their third. They also have a daughter. Her name is Harper.
6 Salma Hayek has a daughter.
7 Lily-Rose Depp's mother is Vanessa Paradis.
8 Prince Harry (Prince Henry of Wales) has a famous grandmother. She is Elizabeth, the Queen of England!

My World

Reading ❯ Celebrity Families

Question Words
When you take a quiz, read the questions carefully. Pay special attention to question words like *who*, *what*, *how many*, etc. They tell you the type of information you need for the answer.

1 Look at the quiz and answer the questions.
   a. What is the quiz about?
   b. What question words does the quiz use?

2 Do the quiz in pairs. Then check your answers.

3 Work in groups. Answer the questions.
   a. How many Celebrity Masterminds are there in your group?
   b. Which questions are easy? Which are difficult?
   c. Which answer is really surprising?

Vocabulary ❯ Family Members

1 Look at the family tree and complete Frank's sentences.

   a. My mother's brother is my _____.
   b. My cousin's mother is my _____.
   c. My uncle's father is my _____.
   d. My mother's mother is my _____.
   e. My cousin's sister is my _____.

2 Use the prompts to write more sentences about the family in activity 1.
   a. (son) _My father's son is my brother._
   b. (daughter) _____
   c. (husband) _____
   d. (wife) _____
   e. (son) _____

Writing ❯ A Celebrity Family Quiz

1 Work in pairs. Write three questions for a celebrity family quiz.

> What does Miley Cyrus's father do?
> a. He's a singer.   b. He's a doctor.   c. He's an actor.

2 Work in groups. Ask and answer the questions.

Listening ❯ Big Families

1 Listen 🎧29 to the radio program and circle the numbers you hear.

   2   3   4   6   8   9   10   16   18

2 Listen again and write the corresponding numbers.
   a. The Casons have ___ children.
   b. There are ___ boys in the Cason family.
   c. There are ___ girls in the Cason family.
   d. Christi buys ___ kg of beef in the supermarket.
   e. Christi buys ___ kg of chicken in the supermarket.
   f. Jessica has ___ children.

Unit 5   51

Grammar > Have/Has

1 Read the extracts and underline examples of *have* and *has*.

> David has a new job.
> They have eighteen children.
> Jessica doesn't have so many kids.
> The Casons don't have a very big house.
>
> See *Grammar Reference*, page 105.

2 Mark the rules *T* (true) or *F* (false).

a. We use *have* or *has* to express possession. ___

b. We use *has* in affirmative sentences for *I, we, you,* and *they*. ___

c. With *he, she*, and *it* we use *have* in affirmative sentences. ___

d. We make negative sentences with *don't/doesn't have*. ___

3 Correct the false sentences.
_____
_____

4 Complete the text with the correct form of *have*.

Jessica is Christi's eldest daughter. She 1) _____ ten brothers and seven sisters. Her youngest sister, Farryn, and her daughter Charlie were born in the same month! But she doesn't 2) _____ a huge family like her parents. Jessica and her husband Cameron 3) _____ three daughters: Melody, Jaedyn, and Charlie. They don't 4) _____ any sons. They live in Indiana, where her family lives.

Speaking > Our Families

1 Complete the table with your family information.

Relatives	Number
brothers	
sisters	
grandfathers	
grandmothers	
uncles	
aunts	
cousins	

2 Work in groups. Describe your family.

> **Useful Language**
>
> I have one grandfather and two grandmothers.
> I don't have sisters.

Views

Listening > Birthday Celebrations

Note-Taking
Taking notes helps you remember precise information. Listen and record information quickly: use abbreviations, initials, key words, or symbols to represent the ideas clearly.

1 Underline what you do on your birthday.
   a. have a party with your friends
   b. get presents
   c. have a birthday cake with candles
   d. wear special clothes
   e. go to the cinema
   f. have a flag outside your house

2 Listen and match the countries with the pictures.
   a. Denmark   b. USA   c. Vietnam

3 Listen again and take notes about each country's birthday celebration.
   a. Denmark: _____
   _____
   b. USA: _____
   _____
   c. Vietnam: _____
   _____

Pronunciation > Word Stress

1 Listen and circle the correct stress pattern.

Monthly Calendar

a.	b.	c.	d.
January / Jan**u**ary	**Feb**ruary / Feb**ru**ary	**March** / **March**	**A**pril / **A**pril

e.	f.	g.	h.
May / **May**	**June** / **June**	**Ju**ly / Ju**ly**	**Au**gust / Au**gust**

i.	j.	k.	l.
September / Sep**tem**ber	**Oc**tober / Oc**to**ber	**No**vember / No**vem**ber	**De**cember / De**cem**ber

(January circled in a.)

2 Listen again and repeat.

Vocabulary > Months

1 Listen and underline the months you hear.
   a. *November/December*
   b. *March/May*
   c. *October/December*
   d. *December/September*

2 Listen and write the months.
   a. _____
   b. _____
   c. _____
   d. _____

Unit 5 53

Reading > **A Comic Strip**

1 Work in groups. Discuss the questions.
   a. What presents do you get for your birthday?
   b. What do you give your mom or dad for their birthday?

2 Read the comic strip and say if she buys a good present and why.

3 Answer the questions.
   a. What does the girl need? _____
   b. Where do the boy and girl go? _____
   c. Why doesn't the girl buy the jacket? _____
   d. What is the problem with the shirts? _____
   e. Is the hat a good present? Why? _____

Grammar > Demonstrative Pronouns

1 Circle the extracts in the comic strip and complete the rules.

> What about this?   These are on sale.
>
> Oops, that is too big!   Look, those are cool!
>
> See *Grammar Reference*, page 105.

a. We use *this* and _____ to talk about one object.

b. We use _____ and *those* to talk about more than one object.

c. We use *this* and _____ to talk about things that are close.

d. We use *that* and _____ to talk about things that are distant.

2 Look at the comic strip and label the speech bubbles.

a. These are nice guitars.

b. I really want this for my birthday!

c. Charly, check that out!

d. Look at those!

Writing > A Comic Strip

1 Work in pairs. Choose one of the titles for a short comic strip.

a. A Present for Mom

b. What a Disaster!

c. A Great Birthday

2 Plan the scenes in your comic strip. Remember to use *this, that, these,* and *those*.

3 Draw and write your comic strip.

4 Exhibit your comic strip in class.

Out and About

Reading > Genetics

1 Work in pairs. Discuss and mark the sentences T (true) or F (false).

   a. We can find genes inside our bodies. ___
   b. We can see genes with our eyes. ___
   c. Genes determine how we look. ___

2 Read the article quickly and underline the best title.

Genes and Hairstyles

It's All in Our Genes

Big Nose and Mouth

We can change our appearance with makeup or a new hairstyle but our basic characteristics are in our genes. And we inherit these. It's not surprising that somebody is similar to his father, or that a friend has her mom's eyes. This is because we inherit the genes that control our appearance from our birth parents. Suppose that Gary's biological parents both have blond hair. Guess what color Gary's hair is. Yes, that's right—blond. That's because Gary inherits their blond hair genes.

What about eye color? Each person has two color genes for their eyes, one from each birth parent. If the genes are the same color, for example blue, then the person has blue eyes. But when we have two different color genes, one color is dominant. For eyes, the brown gene is dominant.

It's interesting to explore these connections. Think of some people you know. Are they tall or short? Do they have big or small eyes? What about their mouths and noses? Who are these people similar to? Remember: the answer is in the genes!

3 Answer the questions.

   a. Can we change our appearance? _____
   b. Do we only inherit genes from one birth parent? _____
   c. Do we inherit hair genes? _____
   d. Is green the dominant gene for eye color? _____
   e. Do genes only determine eye and hair color? _____

56 Unit 5

Vocabulary > Describing People

1 Label the diagram with the words.

| face   mouth   ears   hair   nose   eyes |

2 Underline the correct options.

Gary is 1) *tall/short*. He has 2) *short/long* hair and 3) *green/brown* eyes. He has a 4) *big/small* nose. He has 5) *big/small* ears.

3 Complete the description of Sally.

Sally is short. She has green 1) _____ and long 2) _____. She has a small 3) _____. She has a big 4) _____.

Listening > Great News!

1 Match the situations with the cards.

2 Listen and circle the card for the situation the people mention.

3 Listen again and match the baby's characteristics with the people.

| M=mom   D=dad   G=grandparents |

a. eyes ___   c. nose ___   e. ears ___

b. mouth ___   d. hair ___

Unit 5 57

Grammar > Possessive 's

1 Find the words *mom, dad,* and *grandparent* in the extracts. Underline the letter that follows them.

> *She has her mom's eyes.*
> *She has her dad's big ears.*
> *She has her grandparents' red hair.*
> See *Grammar Reference,* page 105.

2 Match the phrases with the meanings.

a. her mom's eyes   ___ the big ears of her dad
b. her dad's big ears   ___ the eyes of her mom
c. her grandparents' red hair   ___ the red hair of her grandparents

3 Complete the rules.

| + s | without s |

a. To form the possessive, we put an apostrophe _____ after the noun.

b. If the noun ends in s, we put an apostrophe _____ after the noun.

4 Look at the pictures and complete the sentences.

 Matt
 Oli
 Patty
 Rob
 Sue

a. _____ eyes are blue.
b. _____ hair is red.
c. _____ eyes are brown.
d. _____ nose is big.
e. _____ mouth is small.

Writing > A Survey

> Complete the chart for the people in your family.

	Dad	Mom	Grandmother/ Grandfather
Hair color			
Eye color			
Other characteristic (tall, short, etc.)			

Review

1 Complete the sentences about family members.

   a. My _____ brother is my uncle.
   b. My _____ father is my grandfather.
   c. My _____ mother is my aunt.
   d. My _____ daughter is my mother.
   e. My _____ son is my cousin.

2 Look at the pictures. Complete the descriptions with *this, that, these* or *those*.

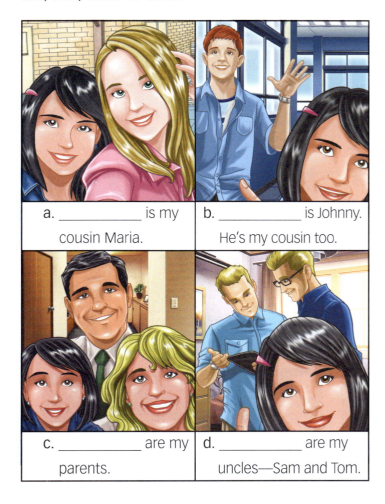

   a. _____ is my cousin Maria.
   b. _____ is Johnny. He's my cousin too.
   c. _____ are my parents.
   d. _____ are my uncles—Sam and Tom.

   > Describe the people in activity 2.

   a. Maria has long hair. She has green eyes.
   b. _____
   c. _____
   d. _____

3 Use your notebook to write a description of a famous person. Ask other students to guess who it is.

4 Listen and write the corresponding months.

   Family Birthdays
   Jamie _____
   Dad _____
   Jean _____
   Mom _____
   Karen _____

   HAPPY BIRTHDAY

5 Read the magazine article.

   ## Who Are You?

   We all have a last name. Your last name is your family name or surname. In some countries people have two last names, one from their father and one from their mother. In English-speaking countries children normally only have their father's last name.

   Last names sometimes give information about a family's history. Some last names tell where a family is from. The last names Brady and Kelly, for example, are very common in Ireland.

   Some families show their identity in other ways. Noble families often have a family emblem. In Scotland, people with the same last name are members of a clan. They wear the clan colors when they attend traditional events.

   > Answer the questions.

   a. How many family names do you have?
   b. Do people in your country change their name when they marry?
   c. Does your last name have a meaning?
   d. Do some families in your country have special emblems?

Unit 5 59

6 Here and There

Value Responsibility Our actions make an impact on the world

1 How responsible are you? Score each area in your life from 5 (very responsible) to 1 (not very responsible).

Arriving at school on time ☐
Participating in class ☐
Doing your homework ☐
Going to bed early ☐

2 Work in pairs. Compare your scores and decide who is more responsible.

Peculiar Jobs

a. I get up and I wash. I don't take a shower because there is no gravity here. Then I eat breakfast. Things float here, so I don't use a cup. I drink coffee from a plastic bag. I exercise after lunch. That's important because human muscles become weak in zero gravity.

b. I live alone but I have a regular routine. I get up early, take a shower and then make breakfast. My kitchen is on the first floor. After breakfast I start work. I walk up 200 steps to check the light. I do that three times a day. I go for a walk after lunch and before I go to bed. I don't exercise in a gym—I don't need to!

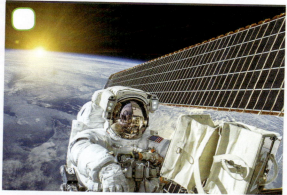

c. I work 12 hours a day. It's very hard work and I'm very tired when I finish. After work, I go back to camp, wash, and eat. The food is excellent. There's isn't much to do during our free time here. I watch movies or read books. I talk to my family by phone every day. I sleep in a small room with five other workers.

60 Unit 6

My World

Reading ❯ Unusual Routines

> **Reading for General Information**
> The first time you read a text, read it quickly to get the general idea. Don't try to understand every word.

1 Read the texts quickly and match them with the pictures.

2 Mark (✓) what the people mention.

Astronaut

a. I take a shower in the morning. ___

b. I drink coffee for breakfast. ___

Lighthouse keeper

c. I work in the morning. ___

d. I exercise in a gym. ___

Oil rig worker

e. I'm tired after I finish work. ___

f. I see my family every day. ___

3 Read the questions and underline the answers in the article.

a. What does gravity stop the astronaut doing?
b. Why is exercise important for astronauts?
c. Where is the kitchen in the lighthouse?
d. How does the lighthouse keeper exercise?
e. Where does the oil rig worker go after work?
f. What does he do in his free time?

Vocabulary ❯ Daily Routines

> Number the activities in the order you do them each day.

___ eat breakfast
___ exercise
___ get up
___ go to bed
___ do homework
___ talk to family
___ take a shower

Writing ❯ A Day in Your Life

> Write a short paragraph for a magazine about your typical day.

Listening ❯ A Visitor to the School

1 Read the questions and mark (✓ or ✗) your answers.

✓ = Yes   ✗ = No

In a typical day, do you...	Me	Jane
eat special food?		
wear a uniform?		
watch TV?		
read?		
listen to music?		

2 Listen and mark (✓ or ✗) the oil rig worker's answers.

3 Listen again and underline the correct information.

a. Jane gets up and *takes a shower/eats breakfast*.
b. She *works/exercises* for twelve hours.
c. She doesn't eat *special food/hamburgers*.
d. She *watches/doesn't watch TV*.

Unit 6   61

Grammar > Simple Present *I, You*

1 Read the extracts and mark the sentences.

✓ = affirmative   ✗ = negative   ? = question

> *I get up and eat breakfast.* ___
> *I don't eat special food.* ___
> *Do you wear special clothes?* ___
> *Yes, I do.* ___
> *Do you watch TV?* ___
> *No, I don't.* ___
>
> See *Grammar Reference,* page 105.

2 Complete the rules.

| do   don't   negative   routines |

a. We use the simple present to talk about _____.

b. We use the auxiliary verb *don't* in _____ sentences.

c. We ask questions with the auxiliary verb _____.

d. We give short answers with the auxiliary verbs *do* and _____.

3 Complete the text with the correct form of the verbs.

| get up   (not) wear   work   (not) work   eat |

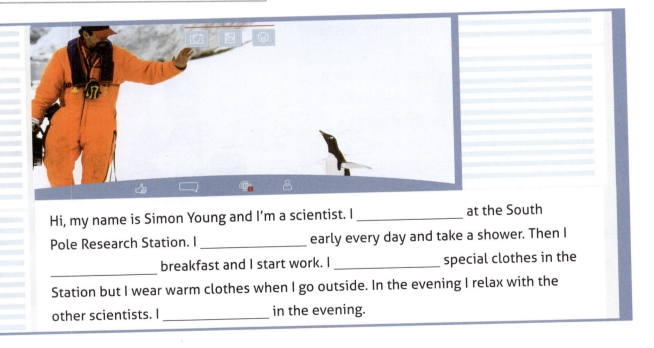

Hi, my name is Simon Young and I'm a scientist. I _____ at the South Pole Research Station. I _____ early every day and take a shower. Then I _____ breakfast and I start work. I _____ special clothes in the Station but I wear warm clothes when I go outside. In the evening I relax with the other scientists. I _____ in the evening.

Writing > Group Routines

> Write six questions to find out what students do in the morning, in the afternoon, and in the evening.

Useful Language

Do you take a shower in the morning?
No, I don't. I take a shower in the evening.

Views

Listening > Keeping Busy

Listening for Key Words
When you want to understand the general idea, listen for key words: nouns and verbs give the most important information.

1 Listen to a radio interview and mark (✓) the correct program.

2 Listen again and write S (Sam) or Z (Zoe) next to activities they like to do.

___ paint pictures   ___ surf the net
___ play a musical instrument   ___ meet friends
___ play soccer   ___ watch movies
___ read books   ___ wash the dishes

Pronunciation > Plurals /s/ vs /iz/

1 Listen and notice the pronunciation of the final -s.

/s/	/iz/
parent - parents	watch – watches
book - books	experience – experiences
tip - tips	wish – wishes

2 Write the plurals of the words in the table according to their pronunciation.

box   brush   cake   class
hat   lip   lunch   photograph

Speaking > Leisure Activities

> Work in groups. Find out what activities people do in their free time.

- play a musical instrument
- paint pictures
- read a book
- surf the net
- meet friends

Useful Language
Do you play a musical instrument in your free time?
Yes, I do. / No, I don't.

Teen Fun
Your 5Qs!

This week we ask Physical Education teacher Ben Cross about Sarah Harper, an excellent young BMX rider.

1 TF: Does Sarah practice every day?
BC: Yes, she does. She cycles to school and she trains in the afternoon.

2 TF: Does she train on weekends?
BC: Yes, she does. She trains on Saturday. She goes to a special sports academy. She doesn't train on Sunday. She relaxes.

3 TF: Does she do other sports?
BC: No, she doesn't. She concentrates on cycling.

4 TF: Does she have free time?
BC: Of course she does! She likes music a lot. She goes to concerts with friends.

5 TF: Does she compete in tournaments?
BC: Yes, she does. She competes in local tournaments three or four times a year. She's very good.

Next week we talk to talented young chess player Martin Doyle. Send your questions to us at 5QS@teenfun.com

Reading > A BMX Rider

1 Read the article and mark (✓) the correct summary.

a. Sarah Cross likes going to concerts in her free time. She is a BMX trainer. She doesn't do other sports. She trains after school. She attends a special sports academy. ___

b. Sarah Harper is a BMX rider. She trains every day after school, and on Saturday she goes to a special music academy. She competes in national tournaments. ___

c. Sarah Harper is a BMX rider. She trains every day, except Sunday. She participates in competitions three or four times a year. She loves music. ___

2 Complete Sarah's weekly agenda.

♥ Weekly Planner ♥

Monday	Tuesday
_____ BMX Training	School _____

Wednesday	Thursday
School _____	_____ BMX Training

Friday	Saturday
_____	_____
	Sunday
	Free

64 Unit 6

Grammar > Simple Present (3rd Person Singular)

1 Read the extracts. Underline the auxiliary verbs and circle the main verbs.

> She trains on Saturday.
> She doesn't train on Sunday.
> Does she cycle every day?
> Yes, she does.
> Does she compete every week?
> No, she doesn't.

See *Grammar Reference,* page 105.

2 Complete the rules.

> does   doesn't   negative   questions   final *s*

a. In affirmative sentences with *he, she,* or *it* we use the main verb with a _____.

b. In _____ sentences we use *doesn't* plus the main verb.

c. We use *does* to make _____.

d. We make short answers with _____ and _____.

3 Complete the article below with the correct form of the verbs.

> cycle   do   go   (not) like   listen
> meet   play   (not) watch

Martin Doyle is a talented young chess player. After school he _____ his bike home and _____ his homework. Then he _____ chess on his computer. He _____ _____ playing sports. On Saturday he gets up early and _____ friends at the local chess club. In the afternoon he _____ to music or _____ to the movies. He _____ _____ much TV.

Writing > A Magazine Article

1 You are going to write a magazine article about your partner. Write five questions to ask.

2 Work in pairs. Take turns asking and answering the questions.

3 Write the article.

Unit 6   65

Out and About

Reading > Journeys to School

1 Answer the questions.
  a. What time do you get up?
  b. How do you get to school?
  c. How long does it take you to get to school?

2 Read the article and underline the times.

What time is it? Time to get up!
by Sara Pathe

There are many ways to get to school, but in some parts of the world this is not so simple. Many primary and secondary students take really long journeys.

Rajit and his friends live in a small village in India. They get up at five o'clock in the morning and walk to school. They walk for two hours. Classes finish at half past one. Rajit and his friends stay at school and study because there is no electricity in their village.

Ju and Lan are from a little village in China. They live on a mountain but their school is in a valley. Every day they go up and down the mountain. They get up at a quarter to six every morning. The children have big school bags and the journey is very long. But they never go alone. "We always take our children to school to help," says Ju's dad. School starts at half past eight in the morning.

3 Match the events to the times.
  a. Ju's school starts.   ___ Five o'clock
  b. Ju and Lan get up.   ___ Half past one
  c. Rajit gets up.   ___ A quarter to six
  d. Rajit's classes finish.   ___ Half past eight

4 Answer the questions.
  a. Where does Rajit live?
  b. Why does Rajit stay at school?
  c. Where is Ju's and Lan's school?
  d. Why does Ju's dad take her and her brother to school?

66   Unit 6

Vocabulary > **Telling the Time**

> Listen and underline the correct times.
  a. It's *7:00/7:15*.
  b. It's *11:10/10:45*.
  c. It's *5:45/4:45*.
  d. It starts at *7:15/7:30*.
  e. I get home at *4:55/5:05*.

Writing > **Going to School**

1 Work in pairs. Ask what time your partner does the activities.
  What time do you…?

get up	
eat breakfast	
go to school	
finish school	
get home	

2 Write about your partner.
  Ana gets up at 7:15.

Listening > **Getting to School**

1 Look at the pictures and say how students are getting to school.

2 Listen to the interview and mark (✓) the photo of the students' journey.

3 Listen again and underline the correct information.
  a. John is a *parent/teacher*.
  b. Students *always/usually* go to school by canoe.
  c. They *sometimes/never* arrive late.
  d. Teachers *never/always* go home on the weekend.

Unit 6 67

Grammar > Simple Present for Routines: We, They, and Adverbs of Frequency

1 Read the extracts. Underline the pronouns and circle the adverbs of frequency.

> Do the students walk to school?
> No, they don't. They never walk.
> They always come by canoe.
> It is sometimes difficult for them to get here.
>
> They sometimes arrive late.
> What about the teachers? Do you live in the school?
> Yes, we do. We always go home on the weekend.

See *Grammar Reference*, page 106.

2 Write the adverbs of frequency on the graph.

never   usually

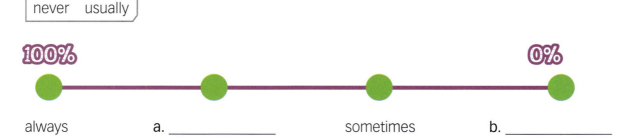

100%   0%

always   a. _____   sometimes   b. _____

3 Circle the correct options.
   a. We use *we* and *they* to refer to *one person/more than one person*.
   b. In questions and negative sentences, we use the auxiliary *do/does* with *we* and *they*.
   c. We normally put adverbs of frequency *before/after* the verb.
   d. We put adverbs of frequency *before/after* the verb *to be*.

4 Complete the text with the correct form of the verbs.

get up   go   leave   (not) live   meet   take   walk

Our names are Dao and Chati. We're brother and sister. We always have a long journey to school. We _____ at 5:00 a.m. and _____ the house at 5:45 a.m. We _____ in the jungle for half an hour. We sometimes _____ our friends Hom and Dang at the river. They _____ in the same village as us. Then we _____ a canoe down the river. We never _____ to school when it rains because the river is very dangerous.

Writing > School Journeys

> Write 4 questions to interview your friends about their journey to school.
   a. _____   c. _____
   b. _____   d. _____

68   Unit 6

Review

1 Match the words.

a. take ___ lunch
b. do ___ a shower
c. go ___ a book
d. eat ___ homework
e. read ___ to bed

2 Work in pairs. Ask and answer questions about Frank and Diana.

	before breakfast	after school	before bed
Frank	always take a shower	sometimes play football	watch TV
Diana	do homework	usually meet friends	listen to music
Frank and Diana	chat online	watch TV	do homework

- *Does Frank take a shower before bed?*
- *Do Frank and Diana watch TV after school?*

3 Write the times you do these activities.

a. get up _____   d. eat lunch _____
b. leave the house _____   e. get home _____
c. arrive at school _____   f. go to bed _____

4 Read the text and underline the tips you follow.

Three Tips for Responsible Teens

by Dr. M. Shelly

It is important for you to take responsibility for your routines. Taking responsibility helps you to be independent. And good habits and routines start in the morning.

Tip 1: Get up in time for school

It is important to be punctual. Never arrive late! It is not polite to make other people wait for you.

Tip 2: Take control of your meals

Do you eat breakfast before school? A good diet is essential for a healthy independent life.

Tip 3: Help at home

It is important to help at home. Do you make your bed? Do you tidy your room? Remember: good habits start at home.

Unit 6 69

7 Food World

Value Self-control Everything in moderation—avoid excess!

1 Mark (✓) the information that is true for you.

I eat/drink this...	in moderation.	in excess.
meat	☐	☐
vegetables	☐	☐
fruit	☐	☐
candy	☐	☐
soda	☐	☐

2 Work in groups. Compare your information and say who has the healthiest diet.

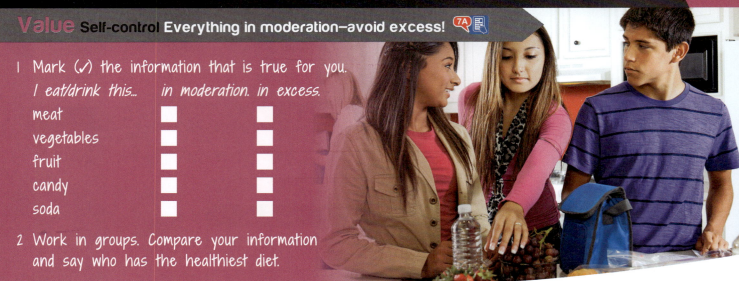

My World

Reading ▸ Where is it from?

Identifying Writer and Audience
When you read a text, ask yourself: Who is the writer? Where is he or she from? Who is the article for? The answers help you understand the content.

1 Look at the article quickly and answer the questions.

a. Who is the writer of the article?
   _____

b. What type of text is it?
   _____

c. Who is the article for?
   _____

Where's your packed lunch from?

By Sam Cooper

Home! That's the simple answer, but look again. Are there any apples? Is there any ham? Where is the bread from? Many students in the US take a packed lunch to school. Their journey varies: some live very close and walk to school, and some others take a bus or car. But how far does the food in a packed lunch travel to get there? Let's take a look!

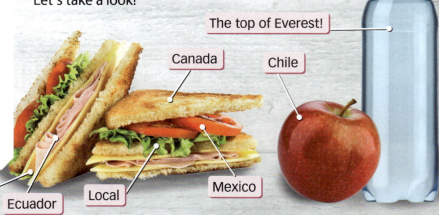

The top of Everest! — Canada — Chile — Argentina — Ecuador — Local — Mexico

Of course it depends what you buy, but nowadays many of the food items in our supermarkets come from other countries. Some food travels thousands of kilometers. In fact, some food from the US travels to another country for processing and then comes back again!

So why not use local food? Using local food helps the local economy. It maintains green and open spaces near you, and it often tastes better because it is fresher. Also, with local food, your poor packed lunch doesn't travel so far!

2 Read the article and complete the table with information from it.

Ways to get to school	Food	Countries

3 Answer the questions.

a. Why does the writer say that "home" is the simple answer?

_____

b. How do the journeys to school of US students vary?

_____

c. Which of the food items in the picture have very long journeys?

_____

d. What are the advantages of using local food?

_____
_____

Vocabulary > Food 7B

1 Classify the food words.

N = Natural   P = Processed

2 Work in pairs. Say your favorite and least favorite food.

3 Find someone in your class with the same food preferences as you.

Useful Language

Do you like cheese? Is it your favorite food?

Listening > A Shopping List

1 Listen and mark (✓) the correct shopping list.

apples
bananas
soda
chocolate

bananas
ham
juice
bread

bananas
ham
cheese
juice

2 Listen again and write the foods the children have at home.

_____
_____

Unit 7   71

Grammar › Some/Any

1 Read the extracts and circle *some* and *any*.

> *There is some cheese.*
> *There isn't any juice.*
> *Are there any apples?*
>
> *Yes, there are some.*
> *Are there any bananas?*
> *No, there aren't any.*
>
> See *Grammar Reference*, page 106.

2 Underline the correct options to complete the rules.

a. We use *some* and *any* to talk about *specified/unspecified* quantities.
b. We generally use *some* in *affirmative/negative* sentences.
c. We generally use *any* in questions and *affirmative/negative* sentences.

3 Look at the food in the refrigerator and complete the conversation with *some* or *any*.

Jon: Diana, can you help me to make a shopping list?
Diana: Sure!
Jon: Are there _____ sodas?
Diana: No, there aren't _____.
Jon: OK. And is there _____ cheese?
Diana: Yes, there is _____.
Jon: What about apples?
Diana: There are _____ and there are _____ bananas too.
Jon: OK, we don't need any fruit then. Do you want to come with me?
Diana: Sorry, I have homework to do.

Speaking › What's in Your Picnic?

> Work in pairs. Choose your favorite picnic.
> Student A: Turn to page 90.   Student B: Turn to page 92.

72 Unit 7

Views

Listening > Food Allergies

Predicting
When you know people are going to talk about a specific topic, think what you know about the topic. This helps you to focus on new information.

1 Work in pairs. Mark (✓) the foods that you think that can give people allergies.

___ peanuts   ___ eggs   ___ cheese
___ milk   ___ bread   ___ apples

2 Listen and label the foods that Jenny and Mark can't eat.

J = Jenny   Mark = M

cheese

eggs

milk

marshmallows

pasta

yogurt

3 Listen again. Mark the sentences T (true) or F (false).

a. Mark doesn't like Chinese food. ___
b. Jenny has an allergy. ___
c. Carol can't eat marshmallows. ___
d. Mark is allergic to dairy products. ___
e. Mark can eat meat and fish. ___

Pronunciation > /ʌ/ vs /uː/

1 Listen to the pronunciation of the underlined sounds.

/ʌ/ pea**nu**t	/uː/ fr**ui**t

2 Listen and write these words in the correct group.

but   you   food   love   run   room

3 Work in pairs. Say the sentences aloud.

a. June loves food.
b. Doug runs in his room.
c. Sue doesn't like peanuts but she loves fruit.

Unit 7   73

Vocabulary > Dishes

1 Label the sign with the names of the dishes.

> hamburger   pancakes   salad
> soup   spaghetti   smoothie

2 Work in pairs. Choose one of the dishes and name some of the ingredients.

3 Compare your answers with other pairs.

Speaking > Food

> Work in pairs. Ask and answer the questions.
> a. What do you have for breakfast/lunch/dinner?
> b. What's your favorite dish?

Reading > Record Breakers

1 Work in pairs. Look at the picture and say what the man is doing.

TODAY'S DISHES

Record Breakers

Some people can do amazing things with food. Have a look at these world records!

I'm sure you can eat it, but can you make pizza? Brian Edler can! He is an extreme pizza maker. He can make 206 medium cheese pizzas in one hour!

How fast can you make breakfast? For sure not like Andrew Robertson. He can make an omelet in 25.24 seconds!

Are you good at sculpting and modeling? Now try with chocolate! Chocolatier Patrick Roger has a world record for a chocolate Christmas tree that is almost 10 meters tall!

So go on, leave your comments and share your talents. What can you do?

Les — OMG! I can't cook, forget make an omelet in less than a minute! I'm good at art, but I don't think I can make a chocolate sculpture. ☹

Sam — My brother is really good at modeling, but can he make a chocolate sculpture? No, he can't!

Aaron — I can't make pizza, but I can eat one large pizza in less than 10 minutes!

2 Read the text to check your answer.

3 Match the people with the information.

a. Brian Edler   large pizza   1 hour
b. Andrew Robertson   one chocolate Christmas tree   25.24 seconds
c. Patrick Roger   one omelet   almost 10 meters tall
d. Aaron   206 medium cheese pizzas   less than 10 minutes

74   Unit 7

Grammar > Can for Ability

1 Read the extracts and underline examples of *can*.

> *He can make an omelet in 25.24 seconds.*
> *I can't cook.*
> *Can he make a chocolate sculpture?*
> *No, he can't.*
> *What can you do?*

See *Grammar Reference*, page 106.

2 Match the questions with the answers.
   a. What do we use *can* to talk about?
   b. Does the main verb change when we use *can*?
   c. How do we make negatives with *can*?
   d. Where do we put the subject in questions with *can*?

   ___ With *can't*.   ___ After *can*.
   ___ Abilities.   ___ No, it never changes.

3 Look at the profiles and complete the interview.

Extreme Teens Casting

Marco		Carla	
skateboard	✓	skateboard	✓
ice-skate	✓	ice-skate	✗
toss pancakes	✓	toss pancakes	✗
spin a pizza	✗	spin a pizza	✓

INTERVIEWER: Hello, Marco. Welcome to our casting.
   What 1) _____ you do?
MARCO: I can 2) _____. I'm really good at skateboarding!
INTERVIEWER: Can 3) _____ ice-skate?
MARCO: 4) _____
INTERVIEWER: What else 5) _____?
MARCO: 6) _____
INTERVIEWER: Good. 7) _____ spin a pizza?
MARCO: 8) _____
INTERVIEWER: OK, thanks for your time.
MARCO: Thanks!

4 Write what Carla can and can't do.
   a. _____
   b. _____
   c. _____
   d. _____

Writing > Abilities Quiz

1 Write a quiz about abilities.

	Yes	No
a. *Can you fry an egg?*		
b. *Can you* _____		
c. _____		
d. _____		
e. _____		

2 Work in pairs. Ask and answer questions.

> **Useful Language**
> *Can you make a pancake?*
> *Yes, I can./No, I can't.*

Unit 7 75

Out and About

Reading > Unusual Restaurants

1 Write the names of any restaurants you know.

2 Read the article and circle the names of the restaurants.

3 Read the article again and underline what is unusual about each restaurant.

4 Write which of the unusual restaurants in the article you would like to try and why.

Crazy Eating Around the World!
By Teresa Curie

When people go on vacation, many like to try the local food. But some restaurants offer an unusual eating experience.

For example, in the Hajime Restaurant in Bangkok, robots—not servers—serve your food. For an uncommon dinner, visit the Dips 'n Stix restaurant in Hamburg, Germany. There you have your plate and napkins, but there are no knives, forks or spoons—you have to eat with your hands.

The Karma Kitchen restaurant in Berkeley, California is unusual in a different way. They have a normal menu with starters, main courses, and desserts, but there is a difference. When you ask for the check, it says "0." In Karma Kitchen restaurants the previous customer pays for your food—and you can pay for the next customer's meal!

Finally, an option to save money is at the Big Texan Steak Ranch in Amarillo, Texas. Here your meal is completely free... when you eat your two-kilogram steak in one hour!

Do you know any unusual restaurants to add to my list? Send me an e-mail! tcurie@aroundtheworld.com

Vocabulary > Eating Out

1 Label the words in the picture.
- a. check
- b. fork
- c. knife
- d. menu
- e. napkin
- f. plate
- g. spoon

2 Complete the sentences.
- a. We use a _____ to eat soup.
- b. Dan is working in a restaurant. He's a _____.
- c. Please cut the cake with this _____.
- d. Please, bring him a _____ of salad.
- e. We're eating sandwiches, we don't need a _____.
- f. Do you want dessert? We have many options in the _____.
- g. Oops, there's sauce on your face. Here's a _____.
- h. It's late. Let's ask for the _____.

Listening > Ordering Food

1 Work in pairs. Look at the pictures on the right and answer the questions.
- a. What type of food do you eat in these restaurants?
- b. What is your favorite type of restaurant?

2 Listen and mark (✓) the restaurant the teenagers go to.

3 Listen again and write what the girl and the boy order.

Girl: _____

Boy: _____

Unit 7   77

Grammar > Offers and Suggestions

1 Read the sentences and label them *O* (offers) or *S* (suggestions).

> *Let's eat something!* ___
>
> *Would you like some cheese with it?* ___
>
> *What would you like?* ___
>
> *What about a pizza?* ___
>
> See *Grammar Reference*, page 106.

2 Complete the rules.

> noun   verb   offers

a. We use *let's* plus a _____ to make a suggestion.

b. We make _____ with *would you*.

c. We make suggestions with *what about* plus a _____.

3 Match the sentence halves.

a. What would   b. What about   c. Would you   d. Let's have

___ a hamburger?

___ a ham and cheese sandwich.

___ you like?

___ like to order?

Speaking > Ordering Food

> Work in pairs. Follow the instructions.
> - Imagine you are in a cafeteria. One of you is the server, the other is the customer.
> - Role-play a conversation.
> - Reverse roles.

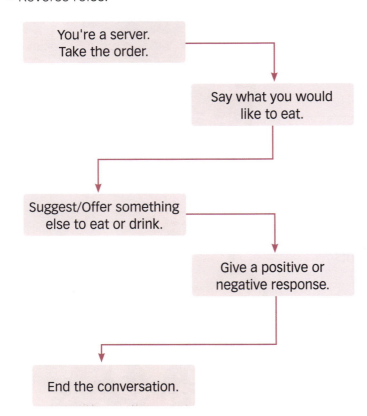

78   Unit 7

Review

1 Find eight food words in the word square.

S	B	R	E	A	D	A	C	Q
P	J	U	I	C	E	N	E	R
M	I	L	K	H	S	T	Y	U
O	O	E	R	E	A	H	R	C
B	N	T	T	E	P	O	P	X
A	A	T	G	S	P	C	R	B
C	O	U	B	E	L	Z	Q	K
O	D	C	K	O	E	J	T	V
N	A	E	G	G	J	T	R	Z

2 Look at the picture. Use your notebook to write questions about four food items.

Are there any bananas on the table?

3 Write four actions.

Actions	Names	Can?

a. Work in groups. Ask what your partners can do and complete the table.
Can you skateboard?
Can you make a chocolate sculpture?
b. Write what your partners can and can't do.

4 Complete the dialogue following the instructions.

WAITER: Hello, _____
   (offer to take the order)
CUSTOMER: _____
   (ask for some food)
WAITER: _____
   (suggest a soup)
CUSTOMER: _____
   (say no)
WAITER: _____
   (suggest something to drink)
CUSTOMER: _____
   (ask for some water)
WAITER: _____
   (offer something else)
CUSTOMER: No, that's all. Thanks!

5 Read the article and answer the questions.

How can we know if we are eating and drinking too much? The answer is in the number of calories we consume.

Calories measure how much energy food or drink contains. The calories that people need varies. A man needs around 2,500 calories a day and a woman, 2,000; very active people need more calories.

Many people consume too many calories. In the US, for example, the average person consumes about 3,641 calories a day. It is important to eat and drink moderate quantities if you want to stay healthy.

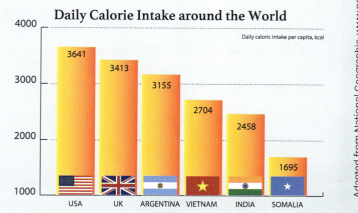

Adapted from National Geographic. www.nationalgeographic.com

a. What happens when we eat too many calories?
b. How can self-control help us to be healthy?

Unit 7 79

8 Home, Sweet Home

Value Helping out Helping others is the secret to a happy life

1 Work in pairs. Answer the questions.
Do you…
a. wash the dishes at home?
b. help family when they are tired?
c. offer help to people you don't know?

2 Mention ways you help others.

Chicago Post

LOCAL INTERNATIONAL ENTERTAINMENT MONEY TRAVEL BLOG

Science Fair

Students at Chicago High are holding their annual Science Fair at the moment. This year's fair is presenting inventions that help around the home. Students are showing different inventions to help make the bed, set the table, or take out the trash.

A fair organizer explains: "Nobody enjoys doing chores but they are very important. This year's fair presents different technologies that can help us keep our homes clean and tidy."

One group of students is working on a home chores app. It is called CHAP. App inventor Sandra Lopez tells us more. "CHAP gives you tasks to do and checks that you do them. There is a schedule with chores and dates for their completion. The app sends you reminders to do the chores."

The app has links to websites with useful tips too. And when you finish the chores, the app rewards you by playing your favorite music!

Visit the Science Fair and see more projects to help in our homes. It's a fun and interesting experience!

‹ PREVIOUS 1 … 13 14 **15** 16 17 … 35 NEXT ›

My World

Reading ▸ A Science Fair

Asking and Answering Questions
When you read a text, ask yourself questions: *Who* does the text mention? *What* is happening? *Where* is it happening? *When* is it happening?

1 Circle what you read online.
   a. social media
   b. news sites
   c. magazines

2 Look at the news site and mark (✓) the topic of the story.
   a. An international science fair ___
   b. A science fair at a local high school ___
   c. A science fair about travel and transport ___

3 Complete the notes about the app.

   a. Name of the app _____
   b. Inventor _____
   c. What the app does _____
   _____
   d. App rewards _____

Vocabulary ▸ House Chores

1 Mark (✓) what you do at home.

	You	Your Partner
tidy up your bedroom		
make your bed		
wash the dishes		
water the plants		
take out the trash		
set the table		

2 Work in pairs. Interview each other and mark your answers in the chart of the activity 1.

Useful Language
Do you tidy up your bedroom?

Listening ▸ What are you doing?

1 Decide which of the science fair projects is the most interesting.
   a. A robot that picks trash up off the floor
   b. An app that helps recycle old clothes
   c. A recycling machine

2 Listen 🎧 and match the projects to the students.

   Student 1 ___
   Student 2 ___
   Student 3 ___

3 Listen again and underline the correct answers.
   a. In conversation 1, what materials is the student recycling?
      1) Paper.
      2) Plastic.
      3) Paper and plastic.
   b. In conversation 2, what does the visitor want to do?
      1) See the robot in action.
      2) Operate the robot.
      3) Buy the robot.
   c. In conversation 3, what does the visitor think the student is doing?
      1) Making an app.
      2) Making a website.
      3) Making clothes.

Unit 8   81

Grammar > Present Continuous *I, You*

1 Read the extracts and underline the verbs.

> *What are you doing?*
> *I'm collecting paper and plastic.*
> *I'm not throwing them away.*
> *Are you making a robot? Yes, I am.*
> *Are you making a website? No, I'm not.*
>
> See *Grammar Reference*, page 107.

2 Mark (✓) the correct options to complete the rules.
   a. We use the present continuous to talk about…
      1. an action that is happening right now. ___
      2. an action that always happens. ___
   b. We form the present continuous with…
      1. *to be* in present + verb + *ing*. ___
      2. *to be* in present + verb + *s*. ___
   c. In negatives, we add *not* after…
      1. the verb *to be*. ___
      2. the verb + *ing*. ___
   d. In questions, we use the verb *to be*…
      1. before the subject ___
      2. after the subject. ___

3 Complete the conversation with the words in the box.

| No | you making | I'm | not | are you |

VISITOR: What 1) _____ doing?
STUDENT: 2) _____ making a robot.
VISITOR: Are 3) _____ a robot to help with homework?
STUDENT: 4) _____, I'm 5) _____.

Speaking > A School Project

1 Choose one of the projects.
   a. Collecting old toys to sell for charity
   b. Recycling waste water to water the yard
   c. Growing plants in garbage

> Make notes of ways to implement your project. Work in pairs. Present your project and discuss what you are doing.

Useful Language
Hi, what are you doing?
I'm working on…
That's interesting. Are you…?

82 Unit 8

Views

Listening > DOITALL

Prediction
Based on the context, you can usually predict the message and language you will hear. Use the pictures or other information to help you anticipate the message.

1. Look at the advertisement and underline the correct option.
   a. It's an ad for a movie.
   b. It's an ad for online security.
   c. It's an ad for selling homes.

2. Listen to the radio ad to check. Circle the feature that is not mentioned.

3. Listen again and mark the statements *T* (true) or *F* (false).
   a. The smart refrigerator can order food for you. ___
   b. The temperature sensors only work at night. ___
   c. The yard robot only waters the plants. ___
   d. The central security system locks all the doors and windows. ___

Vocabulary > Places in A House

1. Label these places in the ad.

   | dining room   bedroom   garage |
   | yard   kitchen   living room |

2. Write a letter to a friend asking what rooms he/she has in his/her house.

Useful Language

Do you have a yard in your house?
How many bedrooms do you have in your house?

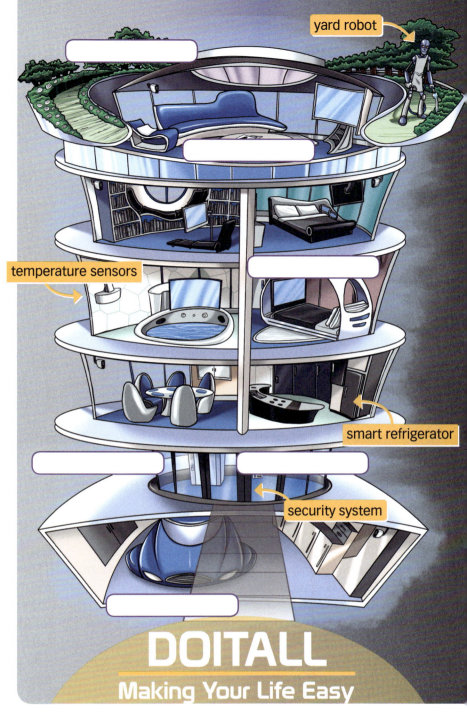

Pronunciation > /b/ vs /v/

1. Listen to the pronunciation of the sounds underlined.
   /b/ <u>b</u>edroom   /v/ li<u>v</u>ing room

2. Listen and write /b/ or /v/ according to the sound you hear at the beginning of each word.
   a. ___   c. ___   e. ___   g. ___
   b. ___   d. ___   f. ___   h. ___

3. Listen and say the sentences.
   a. Victor's bedroom is very big.
   b. Val's best vest is blue.
   c. Bart and Vivian have a beautiful boat.

Unit 8   83

Reading > RX90

1 Read the book summary and mark (✓) the genre.

___ comedy

___ science fiction

___ romance

The Rebellion Zeke Miller

Home   Literature   Book Summary

In Zeke Miller's new book "The Rebellion" it is 2090 and all homes have house robots. The robots do the cleaning and make the food. People use them as slaves. They work all day and never stop. A powerful controller manages the robots. But one day one robot changes everything…

◀ Previous   Next ▶

THE REBELLION
Zeke Miller

2 Read the extract to check. How do you think the robot changes everything?

Danni Turner is at home. She is looking for her house robot. She goes into the living room. RX90 is standing by the window. It isn't moving.
"What are you doing?" Danni asks.
RX90 says nothing.
"That's strange," Danni thinks. She calls the controller.
"How can I help you?"
"There's a problem with my RX90. It isn't cleaning or cooking… It's only standing and looking out of the window."
"Is it recharging?"

"No, it isn't."
"That's strange." The controller presses a button. "What is it doing now?"
"Nothing!" Then he puts Danni on hold. Suddenly, the robot turns to Danni. It is talking…
The controller isn't listening, he is asking for help. RX90 is saying the same words over and over "No more… no more…"
"Turn it off! Turn it off now! Can you hear me?" Danni shouts on the phone.
The call ends suddenly and there is a strange silence…

3 Answer the questions.

a. What is the name of the rebel robot? _____

b. Where is it? _____

c. Why does Danni call the controller? _____

d. What happens when the controller tries to turn the robot off? _____

Grammar > Present Continuous (3rd Person Singular)

1 Read the extracts and underline the verb *to be*.

> She is looking for her house robot.
> The controller isn't listening.
> What is it doing now?
> Is it recharging?
> No, it isn't.

See *Grammar Reference*, page 107.

2 Answer the questions.
For present continuous with *he*, *she*, or *it*...

a. What forms of *to be* do we use? _____
b. What form does the main verb have? _____
c. How do we form negative sentences? _____

3 Use the prompts to label the robots.
a. XZ67 / do the shopping
b. XZ34 / play soccer
c. XZ33 / tidy up the bedroom
d. XZ89 / water the plants
e. XZ51 / wash the dishes

4 Use the prompts in activity 3 to write sentences.

a. XZ67 is doing the shopping.
b. _____
c. _____
d. _____
e. _____

Writing > Picture Description

> What is happening in the picture? Use your notebook to write what is happening. Include the dialogue between the controller and the policeman.

Speaking > Who's That?

> Work in pairs. Play *Who's That?*
Student A: Turn to page 91.
Student B: Turn to page 93.

Unit 8

Out and About

Reading > **No Chairs!**

1. Read the article quickly and circle the best summary.
   a. What to do when you visit a Japanese family
   b. Why we don't need chairs in our houses
   c. Some ways houses are different around the world

HOME | SITEMAP | CONTACT

Be My Guest

When you visit other people's houses it is common to have a chair and table to sit at and eat, and a bed to sleep in. But that is not true everywhere...

In many Arab countries, traditional houses do not have tables or chairs. People take off their shoes before they enter the house. They don't have sofas, they sit on rugs on the floor. They eat sitting on the floor too.

In many Japanese houses, people don't sleep in beds. They use a futon. Tokyo is a very densely populated city and most houses are quite small. The Japanese are very good at using space. During the day they roll up the futon and put it in a closet. That way they can use the bedroom as a living space.

Do you have space problems in your house? Do you think you can eat or sleep like the Arab or Japanese people?

2. Read the article again. Underline what is different from your country.

3. Answer the questions.
   a. What do people do before they go into a traditional Arab house? _____
   b. Where do people eat in an Arab house? _____
   c. Where do people sleep in Japanese houses? _____
   d. Why do people in Japan use futons? _____

Vocabulary > Furniture

1 Label the pictures.

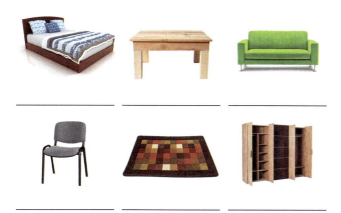

2 Classify the furniture.

Kitchen	Living Room
Bedroom	**Dining Room**

Writing > House Rules

1 Look at the notice and underline the best definition.

A homestay is…

a. a place to leave pets when you go on vacation.

b. an international hotel.

c. a private house where people stay.

Dario's Homestay

Important

To all guests
Please follow these house rules:

* Make your bed in the morning.
* Put your clothes in the closet.
* Clean the table after you eat.

2 Write four more rules for the homestay.

_____
_____
_____
_____

Listening > Helping at Home

1 Work in pairs. Say what is happening in the pictures.

2 Listen and match the conversations with the pictures.

Conversation 1 ___

Conversation 2 ___

Conversation 3 ___

3 Listen again and underline the correct option.

a. James is in the *bedroom/kitchen*.

b. His mom wants help in the *bedroom/kitchen*.

c. Diana is in the *bedroom/bathroom*.

d. Her mom wants help in the *living/dining* room.

e. John is in the *kitchen/yard*.

f. His mom wants help in the *living/dining* room.

Unit 8 87

Grammar > *Can* for Requests

1 Read the extracts and answer the questions.

> *Can you help me in the kitchen, please? (1)*
> *Yes, sure. (2)*
> *Can you tidy up the dining room, please? (3)*
> *Sorry, I can't. (4)*
> *I'm working with dad. (5)*
>
> See *Grammar Reference,* page 107.

Which of the sentences...

a. ask for help? ___, ___

b. gives a negative response? ___

c. gives a positive response? ___

d. makes an excuse? ___

2 Unscramble the conversations.

Conversation 1

___ Sorry, I can't. I'm doing homework.

___ I'm in the living room.

_1_ Tom! Where are you?

___ OK, don't worry.

___ Can you water the plants, please?

Conversation 2

___ Yes, sure... Give me a minute. I'm making my bed.

___ I'm in my bedroom.

___ Can you help me in the yard, please?

___ OK, love. Thanks.

_1_ Julie! Where are you?

Conversation 3

___ Thanks a lot!

___ Where do you want them?

_1_ Can you help carry the shopping?

___ Of course.

___ Put them in the kitchen, please.

Speaking > Asking for Help

> Work in pairs. Use the photos to ask for help and respond.

a.

b.

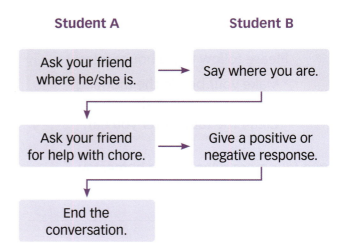

Review

1 Match the words.

   a. make   ___ your room
   b. tidy up   ___ the dishes
   c. water   ___ the table
   d. set   ___ your bed
   e. wash   ___ the plants

2 Look at the pictures and correct the sentences in your notebook.

   a. Joanne is reading in her bedroom.
   b. Chuck is playing the guitar in the living room.
   c. Dad is tidying up the bathroom.
   d. Riley is doing her homework in the kitchen.
   e. Mom is watering plants in the garage.

3 Read the social media post and answer the questions.

Glenn

What do you do to help others?

Griselda MV I love animals but these aren't my dogs. My neighbors can't leave their homes: Maria is 88, George is 90, and Oscar is 92. I'm taking their dogs to the park today. I like to help. Sometimes I do the shopping. Not a lot — just small things. My neighbors don't pay me. I do this for free. It makes me happy to help people.

a. What is Griselda doing in the photo?

_____

b. Why is she doing this?

_____

c. Does Griselda get money for what she does?

_____

d. How do people help the elderly in your community?

_____

Unit 8   89

Student A

Pairwork

Unit 2 (page 28)

Useful Language
Hi, I want to register for the karate club.
Great! What's your…?
How old are you?

1. Look at the registration form and think of a club you want to join.

Charleston Community Center Registration Form

Club: _____
First name: _____
Last name: _____
Age: _____
Phone number: _____
E-mail address: _____
School: _____

@ = at
. = dot
- = dash
/ = slash

2. Work in pairs. Answer your partner's questions.
3. Reverse roles.

Unit 7 (page 72)

Useful Language
Are there any apples?
Is there any juice?

1. Ask your partner questions to find what food he or she has in his or her picnic.

2. Answer your partner's questions about your picnic.

3. Say which picnic you prefer and why.

   I prefer picnic A. I don't like picnic B because there isn't any juice. I love juice.

Student A

Unit 8 (page 85)

Useful Language
There's a man wearing a...
A woman is dancing.

1 Play *Who's That?*

   a. Look at the picture for twenty seconds and then close your book.

   b. Work in pairs. Take turns describing the people. Award one point for every correct description.

   There's a woman with a blue hat. — Wrong, it's a man. Look!
   A man is making a call. — Correct, one point!

   c. The student with the most points wins the game.

Pairwork 91

Student B

Pairwork

Unit 2 (page 28)

Useful Language
Hi, I want to register for the karate club.
Great! What's your…?
How old are you?

1. You work at Charleston Community Center. Look at the registration form and prepare questions to register your partner for a club.

Charleston Community Center Registration Form

Club: _____
First name: _____
Last name: _____
Age: _____
Phone number: _____
E-mail address: _____
School: _____

@ = at
. = dot
- = dash
/ = slash

2. Work in pairs. Ask questions to complete the registration form with your partner's information.

3. Reverse roles.

Unit 7 (page 72)

Useful Language
Are there any apples?
Is there any juice?

1. Answer your partner's questions about your picnic.

2. Ask your partner questions to find what food he or she has in his or her picnic.

3. Say which picnic you prefer and why.

I prefer picnic A. I don't like picnic B because there isn't any juice. I love juice.

92 Pairwork

Student B

(page 85) **Unit 8**

Useful Language

There's a man wearing a…
A woman is dancing.

1 Play *Who's That?*

  a. Look at the picture for twenty seconds and then close your book.
  b. Work in pairs. Take turns describing the people. Award one point for every correct description.
  There's a woman with a blue hat. — Wrong, it's a man. Look!
  A man is making a call. — Correct, one point!
  c. The student with the most points wins the game.

Pairwork 93

Project 1 ⌄ A Phrasebook

> Mark (✓) what you use when you learn English.

a. a dictionary ☐
b. pens ☐
c. a computer ☐
d. a smartphone ☐
e. songs ☐
f. a course book ☐
g. a notebook ☐

a.

⌄ Analyze

- Mark the parts of English that are easy and difficult for you. It is important to record and concentrate on difficult parts.

	☺ easy ☹ difficult
Pronunciation	
Grammar	
Vocabulary	

- Look at the four phrasebooks and answer the questions.
    1. What information do they contain?
    2. How are they similar?
    3. How are they different?

⌄ Evaluate

b.

- Choose a phrasebook that is interesting for you. Evaluate it.

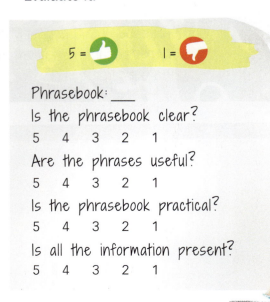

5 = 👍   1 = 👎

Phrasebook: ___
Is the phrasebook clear?
5 4 3 2 1
Are the phrases useful?
5 4 3 2 1
Is the phrasebook practical?
5 4 3 2 1
Is all the information present?
5 4 3 2 1

94 Projects

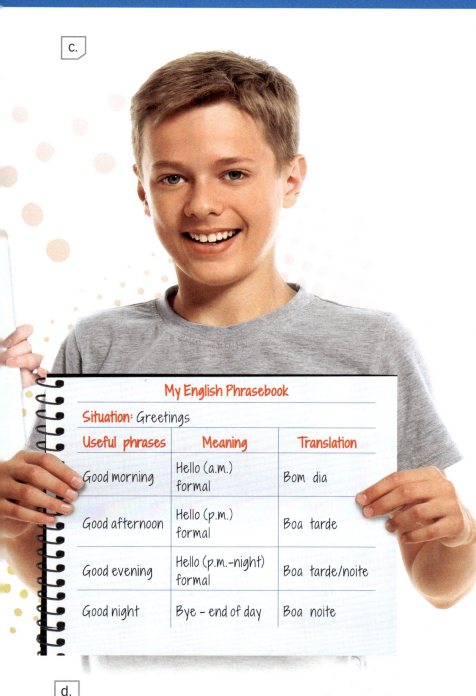

c.

d.

Prepare

- Create a phrasebook to record vocabulary and phrases. Follow the steps.

  Step 1: Decide on the technology for the phrasebook: notebook, smartphone, tablet (audio, video, written), etc.

  Step 2: Decide how to organize the phrasebook: translation, notes, illustrations, phrases, pronunciation, verb tables, etc.

Write a First Draft

- Plan and write the vocabulary and phrases for part 1 of your phrasebook.

Edit Your Work

- In groups, evaluate each other's work. Make suggestions for improvements.

Write a Final Draft

- Write a final version of part 1 of your phrasebook.

Create a Product

- Organize the sections of the phrasebook in a logical order (alphabetical, thematic, course book order, etc.).
- Make final changes.

Present

- Present your phrasebook to the class.
- Remember: add new phrases to your phrasebook during the year!

Projects 95

Project 2 ⌄ A Country Poster

1 Choose a country that is interesting for you. Complete the information about that country.
Country
Capital
Colors of the flag
Language(s)

2 Work in groups. Share your information.

⌄ Analyze

- Look at the poster. Underline the information it includes.
  a country map
  famous people
  geography photos
  history
  interesting places
  politics

- Read the Facts in Brief and underline the information used in the poster.

Facts in Brief: Uruguay

Capital Montevideo

Official Language Spanish

Official Name República Oriental del Uruguay (Eastern Republic of Uruguay).

Area 68,037 mi² (176,215 km²)

Population Current estimate—3,416,000; density, 50 per mi² (19 per km²); distribution, 93% urban, 7% rural

National Anthem *Himno nacional del Uruguay* ("National Anthem of Uruguay")

Flag Uruguay's flag and coat of arms were adopted in 1830. The flag has nine horizontal alternating stripes of blue and white. The sun is a symbol of independence.

Currency Uruguayan peso; one hundred centésimos equal one peso

Government Constitutional republic

Climate Mild and wet

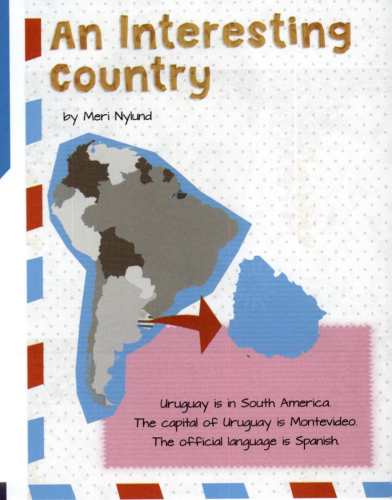

An Interesting Country
by Meri Nylund

Uruguay is in South America. The capital of Uruguay is Montevideo. The official language is Spanish.

⌄ Evaluate

- Use the questions to evaluate the school project.

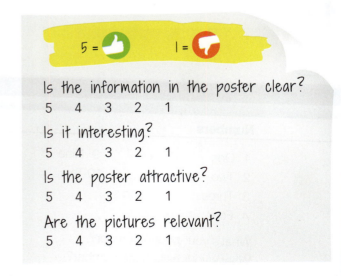

5 = 👍   1 = 👎

Is the information in the poster clear?
5 4 3 2 1

Is it interesting?
5 4 3 2 1

Is the poster attractive?
5 4 3 2 1

Are the pictures relevant?
5 4 3 2 1

- Work in groups to discuss how to improve the poster.

96 Projects

The Uruguayan flag is white and blue with a yellow sun.

There are many famous Uruguayans. Luis Suarez is a fantastic footballer; Natalia Oreiro is an actress; Juan Carlos Onetti is a famous writer. In 2005, the singer and songwriter Jorge Drexler won the Academy Award for the Best Original Song.

Uruguay is a beautiful country. Some interesting places are the Rambla in Montevideo and Punta del Diablo, 5 km from the city.

▼ Prepare

- Work in groups. You are going to create a poster about a country. Follow the steps.
  Step 1: Choose a country.
  Step 2: Decide what information to include.
  Step 3: Divide into pairs and work on a section of the poster.
  Step 4: Research the information and images for your section.

▼ Write a First Draft

- In your pair, write your section of the poster. Select the images to include.

▼ Edit Your Work

- In your group, evaluate and correct each section. Use the questions as a guide.
  1. Is the spelling and punctuation correct?
  2. Is the vocabulary correct and appropriate?
  3. Is the grammar correct?
  4. Is the information clear?
  5. Are the images appropriate?

▼ Write a Final Draft

- Rewrite your section of the poster to include the corrections.

▼ Create a Final Product

- Make any final changes.
- Organize the sections of the poster into a logical order.
- Add images and design.
- Prepare a presentation.

▼ Present

- Present and display your poster to the class.
- Answer questions from the class.

Project 3 ▾ A Family Scrapbook

1 Write three interesting facts about a person who is special to you in your family.

2 Work in groups. Say why your person is special.

▾ Analyze

- Look at Adede's family scrapbook. Circle the information she includes.
  1. Names
  2. Places
  3. Favorite activities
  4. Routines
  5. Dates
  6. Jobs

- Write what these numbers and dates refer to in the scrapbook.
  1. 16 _____
  2. 40 _____
  3. 67 _____
  4. 61 _____

- Underline examples of family members and possessive adjectives.

▾ Evaluate

- Use the questions to evaluate the scrapbook.

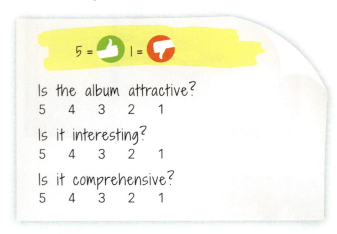

5 = 👍 1 = 👎

Is the album attractive?
5 4 3 2 1

Is it interesting?
5 4 3 2 1

Is it comprehensive?
5 4 3 2 1

- Discuss how to improve the scrapbook. Add ideas of other information to include.

FAMILY MATTERS!

This is where I live with my family.

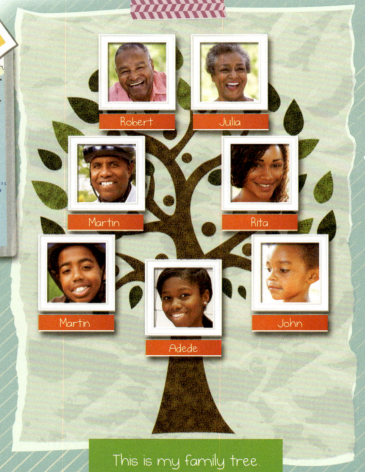

This is my family tree.

98 Projects

Prepare

- Work in groups. You are going to create a Family Scrapbook.
  1. Decide what information to include in the scrapbook.
  2. Collect photos to include in your scrapbook.
  3. Show the photos to your colleagues. Say why they are important to you.

Write a First Draft

- Write a first draft of the scrapbook. Give information about your photos but don't glue them.

Edit Your Work

- Show your scrapbook to other students in your class. Ask them for comments and corrections. Use the questions as a guide.
  1. Is the scrapbook attractive?
  2. Is it interesting?
  3. Is the language correct?

Write a Final Draft

- Prepare the final draft of your scrapbook. Glue photos and any other necessary elements.

Present

- In your class, present the individual scrapbook.
- Display your scrapbook around the classroom.

These are my grandparents. My grandfather is a doctor. He is 67 and my grandmother is 61.

March 23 is my mom's birthday. She's 40. He's my brother Martin. He's the youngest of the family.

Here is my brother with my dad. They love cycling!

These are my friends. We're all 16. We play on a volleyball team.

Project 4 A Weekend Eating Plan

> Work in groups. Discuss the questions.
> a. Which meals do you eat together as a family?
> b. Who decides the menu in your house?

Analyze

- Classify the foods on the Eating Plan into the Food Pyramid categories.

Fats, Oils, and Sweets	
Milk, Meat, and Fish	
Vegetables and Fruits	
Bread, Pasta, Cereals, and Rice	

- Look at the Food Pyramid below and suggest ways to make the eating plan more balanced.

- Answer the questions.
  1. Which of the foods on the menu does your family eat on the weekend?
  2. What other foods do you eat on the weekend?

Evaluate

- Work in groups. Discuss the questions

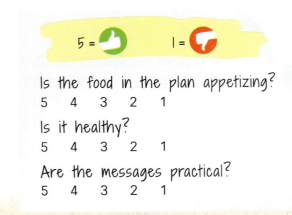

Is the food in the plan appetizing?
5   4   3   2   1

Is it healthy?
5   4   3   2   1

Are the messages practical?
5   4   3   2   1

- Suggest ways to improve the plan.

FOOD PYRAMID
- FATS, OILS, AND SWEETS
- MILK, MEAT, AND FISH
- VEGETABLES AND FRUITS
- BREAD, PASTA, CEREALS, AND RICE

* Eat fruit every day.
* Don't eat meat every day!
* Don't forget to brush your teeth after you eat!

Weekend Eating Plan

Saturday 7/21

Breakfast	Lunch	Dinner
cereal	chicken	omelet
milk	potatoes	salad
apple	carrots	bread
water	yogurt	

Sunday 7/22

Breakfast	Lunch	Dinner
toast	hamburger	pizza
orange juice	french fries	ice cream
banana	soda	

Research

- You are going to create a weekend eating plan for your family. Follow the steps.

  Step 1: Research different meals (breakfast, lunch, dinner)

  Step 2: Find information about healthy options for your meals. Take notes.

Prepare

- Choose which dishes you are going to include in your plan.
- Make a list of useful messages to go with your plan. Classify the ingredients into the food pyramid and make sure the meal is balanced.

Write a First Draft

- Write a first draft of your plan and the messages.

Edit your Work

- Read, analyze, and correct your work.

Write a Final Draft

- Write a clean version of your plan and the messages. Include pictures if you want.

Present

- Display your weekend eating plan and the messages.
- Take a class vote on the best plan. Use these suggestions as a guide.
    1. how healthy the plans are
    2. how useful the messages are
    3. how attractive the presentation is

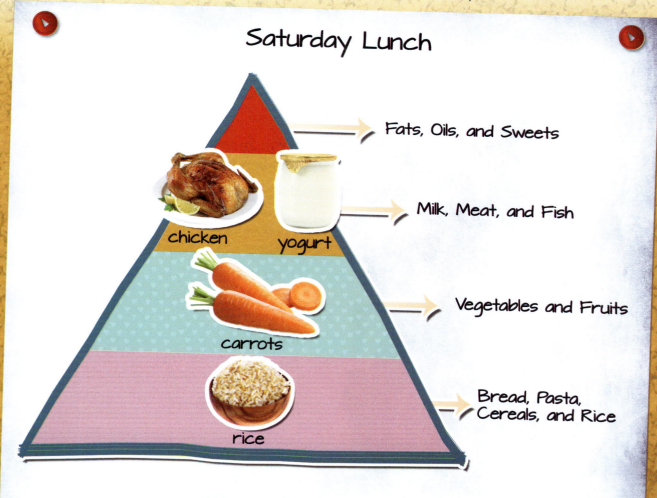

Grammar Reference

Unit 1

Greetings (See page 12)

Use

- We use greetings to say hello, respond to greetings, or to say good-bye.
  Good morning.
  Nice to meet you.
  Hello.
  Good-bye!
  See you later.
  How are you?
  Fine thanks, and you?

Classroom Language (1) (See page 15)

Use

- We use classroom language to make polite requests or give instructions.
  Listen for your name.
  Sit down.
  Take out your books.
  May I come in?
  May I borrow a book?

Classroom Language (2) (See page 18)

Use

- We also use classroom language to ask for information.
  What does "match" mean?
  How do you say escrever in English?
  Can you repeat that?
  I don't understand.

Unit 2

Possessives *My/Your* (See page 22)

Use

- We use possessives to express ownership or a close personal relationship.
  My name is Jenny.
  The Dallas Cowboys are my favorite team.
  What's your favorite sport?

To be 1st and 3rd Person (See page 25)

Use

- We use the verb **to be** in the simple present tense to give information about people or things.
  My name is Pamela.
  I'm 15.
  She's from Texas too.

Form

Affirmative

| I | am (I'm) | |
| He She It | is (He's/She's/It's) | from the US. |

To be 2nd Person (Questions and Short Answers) (See page 28)

Use

- We use the verb **to be** in questions to find out information about people or things.
  Are you a student?
  Yes, I am.
  Are you from the US?
  No, I'm not

Form

Questions

| Are | you | at high school? from Larkston? |

Short Answers

| Are you a student? | Yes, I am. No, I am (I'm) not. |

102 Grammar Reference

Unit 3

Simple Present *To be* 3rd Person (Questions and Short Answers) (See page 32)

Use

- Questions can begin with question words: **what, where, which, how, who, when**.
  Where is Rita Ora from?
  Where is Ryan Reynolds from?
- The answer to questions without a question word is **yes** or **no**.
  Is he from Australia?
  No, he isn't.
  Is your family from India?
  Yes, it is.

Form

Questions

Where	is	he she it	from?

Short Answers

Is he/she/it from New York?	Yes, he/she/it is. No, he/she/it is not (isn't).

Simple Present *To be* (Plurals) (See page 35)

Use

- We use the verb **to be** in the simple present tense plural to give or find out information about people or things.
  They're beautiful too.
  We aren't professional dancers.
  Are your clothes special?
  Yes, they are.

Form

Affirmative and Negative

We You They	are (We're/You're/They're) are not (aren't)	from Bahia.

Short Answers

Are we/you/they singers?	Yes, we/you/they are. No, we/you/they are not (aren't).

Question Words (See page 38)

Use

- We use question words to ask specific information about people or things.
  1. We use **who** to ask about people.
  2. We use **where** for places.
  3. We use **how** for manners or ways.
  4. We use **what** for things.
  Who is the father of American independence?
  Where is Mount Rushmore?
  How do you spell Rushmore?
  What's the capital of the US?

Grammar Reference 103

Grammar Reference

Unit 4

There is/There are (See page 42)

Use

- We use **there is/there are** to say that something exists.
  There is a 200 km bike network in the city.
  There aren't beaches in Canberra.
  Is there a fishing area?
  Yes, there is.

Form

Affirmative and Negative

There	is (There's) is not (isn't)	a lake.
	are are not (aren't)	markets in Melbourne.

Short Answers

Is there a market near your hotel?	Yes, there is. No, there is not (isn't).
Are there kangaroos?	Yes, there are. No, there are not (aren't).

Articles a/an/the (See page 45)

Use

- We use articles to define nouns as specific or unspecific.
- We use **a/an** to talk about singular nouns that are unspecific. We use **an** with singular nouns that have an initial vowel sound (elephant, animal, etc.)
  You can have a quick snack.
  Enjoy an animal adventure.
- We use **no article** with plural or uncountable nouns that are general or unspecific.
  There are taxis everywhere in Sidney.
  There are showers for surfers.
- We use **the** when we talk about something more certain or specific.
  The station is near the park.
  Where do you take the ferry?

Directions (See page 48)

Use

- We use imperatives to give directions.
  Go straight.
  Turn right.

Form

- We don't say **you** and we use the verb in the base form.

Affirmative

Turn left.
Go past Bondi Park.

104 Grammar Reference

Unit 5

Have/Has (See page 52)

Use

- We use **have/has** to show possession.
  David has a new job.
  They have eighteen children.
  She doesn't have so many kids.
  The Casons don't have a very big house.

Form

Affirmative

I	have	
He She	has	a very big house.
We You They	have	

Negative

I	do not (don't)		
He She	does not (doesn't)	have	a huge family.
We You They	do not (don't)		

Demonstrative Pronouns (See page 55)

Use

- We use **this, these, that,** and **those** in the place of a noun to show proximity.
  What about this?
  Oops, that is too big!
  These are on sale.
  Look, those are cool!

Form

- We use **this** (singular) and **these** (plural) for people or things near us.
  I really want this for my birthday!
  These are nice guitars.

- We use **that** (singular) and **those** (plural) for people or things that are not near us.
  Charly, check that out!
  Look at those!

Possessive 's (See page 58)

Use

- We add **'s** to nouns to show possession.
  It's a photo of my sister's new baby.
  What color is your dad's hair?
  She has her grandparents' red hair.

Form

- We add **'s** to singular nouns and just **'** to plural nouns that end in –s.
  Her dad's big ears
  Her grandparents' red hair

Unit 6

Simple Present *I, You* (See page 62)

Use

- We use the simple present to indicate an action that happens over a long period or is a regular, habitual activity.
  I get up and eat breakfast.
  I don't eat special food.
  Do you watch TV?
  No, I don't.

Form

Affirmative and Negative

I You	wear don't wear	special clothes.

Short Answers

Do you exercise?	Yes, I do. No, I do not (don't).

Simple Present (3rd Person Singular) (See page 65)

Form

- The form of the simple present changes for third person singular, adding –**s** to the verb. We make negative sentences by using the auxiliary **does** and **not (doesn't)** before the verb.
  She trains on Saturday.
  She doesn't train on Sunday.
  Does she cycle every day?
  Yes, she does.
  Does she compete every week?
  No, she doesn't.

Affirmative and Negative

He She It	walks doesn't walk	for two hours.

Short Answers

Does he/she/it walk every day?	Yes, he/she/it does. No, he/she/it does not (doesn't).

Simple Present *We, They* (See page 68)

Form

Affirmative and Negative

We They	arrive don't arrive	at seven o'clock.

Short Answers

Do you walk to school?	Yes, we do. No, we do not (don't).
Do they come every day?	Yes, they do. No, they do not (don't).

Unit 7

Some/Any (See page 72)

Use

- We use **some** and **any** to give information about the number of something. We use **some** when the speaker cannot specify or does not need or want to specify a number or an exact amount. We use **any** for negatives and questions.

    *There is **some** cheese.*
    *There are **some** eggs.*
    *Are there **any** apples?*
    *There isn't **any** juice.*

Can for Ability (See page 75)

Use

- We use **can** to express abilities or lack of them.

    *He **can** make an omelet in 25.24 seconds.*
    *I **can't** cook.*
    ***Can** he make a chocolate sculpture?*
    *No, he **can't**.*
    *What else **can** you do?*

Form

Affirmative and Negative

I You He She It We They	can cannot (can't)	skateboard.

Questions

What	can	I you he she it we they	do?

Short Answers

Can you/he/she/it/ we/they spin a pizza?	Yes, I/he/she/it/we/they can. No, I/he/she/it/we/they cannot (can't).

Offers and Suggestions (See page 78)

Use

- We use **Let's…** and **What about…?** to make suggestions. We use **What would you…?** and **Would you…?** to make offers.

    Let's eat something!
    What about a pizza?
    What would you like?
    Would you like some cheese with it?

Form

- We use **Let's** with no subject and followed by the base form of the verb.

    Let's have a ham and cheese sandwich.

- We follow **What about..?** with a noun.

    What about a hamburger?

- We use **What would you…?** and **Would you…?** followed by the base form of the verb.

    What would you like to drink?
    Would you like to order?

Unit 8

Present Continuous *I, You* (See page 82)

Use

- We use the present continuous to describe an action that is happening around this moment in time.

  I'm making a cake.
  I'm not throwing them away.
  Are you throwing out the old books? Yes, I am.
  What are you doing?

Form

- We form the present continuous tense for **I** and **you** with the verb **to be** + the present participle (-ing).

Affirmative and Negative

I	am (I'm) am not (I'm not)	collecting paper and plastic.
You	are (You're) are not (aren't)	

Short Answers

What	are	you	doing?

Are you making a robot?	Yes, I am. No, I am (I'm) not.

Present Continuous (3rd Person Singular) (See page 85)

Form

- We form the present continuous tense for **he**, **she** and **it** with **is** + the present participle (-ing).

  She's looking for her house robot.
  It **isn't** moving.
  Is it recharging?
  No, it **isn't**.

Affirmative and Negative

He She It	is is not (isn't)	doing the shopping.

Questions

What	is	he she it	doing now?

Short Answers

Is he/she/it playing soccer?	Yes, he/she/it is. No, he/she/it is not (isn't).

Can for Requests (See page 88)

Use

- We use **can** in questions to make requests.

  Can you water the plants, please?
  Sorry, I can't.

Numbers, Days of the Week, Months

Numbers	
1	one
2	two
3	three
4	four
5	five
6	six
7	seven
8	eight
9	nine
10	ten
11	eleven
12	twelve
13	thirteen
14	fourteen
15	fifteen
16	sixteen
17	seventeen
18	eighteen
19	nineteen
20	twenty
21	twenty-one
22	twenty-two
23	twenty-three
30	thirty
40	forty
50	fifty
60	sixty
70	seventy
80	eighty
90	ninety
100	one hundred

Days of the Week
Monday
Tuesday
Wednesday
Thursday
Friday
Saturday
Sunday

Months
January
February
March
April
May
June
July
August
September
October
November
December

Alphabet

Alphabet 109

Phonetic Symbols

Consonant sounds		
/p/	as in	pet /pɛt/
/b/	as in	bat /bæt/
/t/	as in	tip /tɪp
/d/	as in	dig /dɪg/
/k/	as in	cat /kæt/
/g/	as in	good /gʊd/
/f/	as in	fit /fɪt/
/v/	as in	van /væn/
/s/	as in	sip /sɪp/
/z/	as in	zip /zɪp/
/l/	as in	lid /lɪd/
/m/	as in	mat /mæt/
/n/	as in	nine /naɪn/
/h/	as in	hat /hæt/
/r/	as in	rat /ræt/
/j/	as in	yes /jɛs/
/w/	as in	win /wɪn/
/θ/	as in	thin /θɪn/
/ð/	as in	the /ðə/
/ʃ/	as in	ship /ʃɪp/
/ʒ/	as in	vision /ˈvɪʒən/
/tʃ/	as in	chin /tʃɪn/
/dʒ/	as in	Japan /dʒəˈpæn/
/ŋ/	as in	English /ˈɪŋglɪʃ/

Vowel sounds		
/i/	as in	very /veri/
/i:/	as in	see /si:/
/ɪ/	as in	bit /bɪt/
/ɛ/	as in	ten /tɛn/
/æ/	as in	stamp /stæmp/
/ɑ/	as in	father /ˈfɑðər/
/o/	as in	sore /sor/
/ʊ/	as in	book /bʊk/
/u:/	as in	you /ju:/
/ʌ/	as in	sun /sʌn/
/ə/	as in	about /əˈbaut/
/ɑ:/	as in	dog /dɑ:g/
/eɪ/	as in	fate /feɪt/
/aɪ/	as in	fine /faɪn/
/ɔɪ/	as in	boy /bɔɪ/
/au/	as in	now /nau/
/ou/	as in	go /gou/
/ɪə/	as in	near /nɪər/
/eə/	as in	hair /heər/

Irregular Verbs

Base form	Simple past	Past participle
be	was/were	been
become	became	become
begin	began	begun
break	broke	broken
bring	brought	brought
build	built	built
buy	bought	bought
catch	caught	caught
choose	chose	chosen
come	came	come
cost	cost	cost
do	did	done
drink	drank	drunk
drive	drove	driven
eat	ate	eaten
fall	fell	fallen
feel	felt	felt
fight	fought	fought
find	found	found
fly	flew	flown
forget	forgot	forgotten
get	got	gotten
give	gave	given
go	went	gone
grow	grew	grown
have	had	had
hear	heard	heard
hit	hit	hit
keep	kept	kept
know	knew	known

Base form	Simple past	Past participle
leave	left	left
lose	lost	lost
make	made	made
meet	met	met
pay	paid	paid
put	put	put
read /ri:d/	read /red/	read /red/
ride	rode	ridden
run	ran	run
say	said	said
see	saw	seen
sell	sold	sold
send	sent	sent
shut	shut	shut
sing	sang	sung
sit	sat	sat
sleep	slept	slept
speak	spoke	spoken
spend	spent	spent
steal	stole	stolen
swim	swam	swum
take	took	taken
tell	told	told
think	thought	thought
throw	threw	thrown
understand	understood	understood
wake	woke	woken
wear	wore	worn
win	won	won
write	wrote	written

Workbook Unit 1

1 Complete the conversations.

a. A: Good evening, Mr. White.

B: _Good evening._

A: How are you?

B: _____

A: Fine thanks! Welcome to Dayton School.

B: _____

b. A: Good afternoon! What's your name?

B: _I'm George Smith._

A: My _name's_____ Charles Davis. Nice to meet you.

B: _____

c. A: Good morning, everyone. I'm Grace Nicholl, your teacher.

B: _____

A: How are you?

B: _____

2 Look at the clocks and complete the expressions with the words in the box.

| night   morning   afternoon   evening |

7:00 a.m.

a. in the _____

10:30 p.m.

3:00 p.m.

c. in the _____

6:15 p.m.

b. at _____

d. in the _____

3 Number the conversation in order.

____ Fine thanks, and you?

____ Fine thanks. See you later, OK?

_1_ Good morning, Mr. Smith.

____ Hello, Tom.

____ How are you?

____ Yes, great. Bye! See you in class.

4 Change the instructions to polite requests.

a. Come in. _May I come in?_____

b. Sit down. _____

c. Stand up. _____

d. Open the window. _____

Workbook Unit 1

5 Unscramble the words to form sentences.

a. close / I / May / door / the _____?

b. go / to / bathroom / May / I / the _____?

c. in / come / I / May _____?

d. your / book / borrow / I / May _____?

6 Look at the images and write the sentences.

a. _____
Sorry, I'm late.

c. _____
It's very noisy.

b. _____
My hands are dirty.

d. A: _____
B: Sure. Of course!

7 Look at the images. Write the correct words.

a. _____

c. _____

e. _____

g. _____

b. _____

d. _____

f. _____

h. _____

Workbook Unit 1

8 Number the dialogue in order.

___ Can you repeat that? I don't understand.

_1_ How do you say *escrever* in English?

___ Sure. Write.

___ Write.

___ Write. Thanks.

9 Write the questions to complete the dialogues.

a. A: _____ ?

B: It means *cadeira*.

b. A: _____ ?

B: You say "library."

c. A: Open the door, please.

B: I don't understand. _____ ?

A: Open the door, please.

10 Look at the pictures and circle the words.

E	W	E	R	A	S	E	R	L	O
W	I	R	T	E	I	S	D	B	V
H	D	Q	C	D	M	P	Z	R	S
B	E	W	A	S	B	Z	W	Y	G
A	S	B	F	Z	I	K	S	A	F
D	K	K	E	C	H	A	I	R	A
F	G	P	T	Z	W	D	Z	Y	R
N	O	T	E	B	O	O	K	L	L
G	I	V	R	V	I	W	C	B	X
S	D	P	I	T	K	Z	S	P	J
B	C	L	A	S	S	R	O	O	M

⌄ Self-Assessment   Unit 1

Think about Unit 1. Write your impressions about each section of the unit.
Include what you learned and how you improved.

Unit Opener

My World

Views

Out and About

⌄ What do I have to do to learn more?

☐ Pay more attention in class.

☐ Do more practice exercises.

☐ Participate more in class.

☐ Study more at home.

☐ Read and listen to English in my free time.

☐ Practice writing and speaking.

☐ Other: _____

Workbook Unit 2

1 **Complete the crossword.**

Across ➔
1 Pau Gasol is a great _____ player.
5 Serena Williams is my favorite _____ player.
6 The Dallas Cowboys are a famous _____ team.

Down ↓
2 You use arms and legs to move through water.
3 Lionel Messi is the best _____ player in the world.
4 You need a bat and a ball to play this sport.

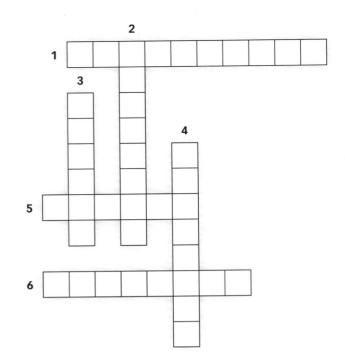

2 **Unscramble the words to form sentences.**

a. A: What's your name?
   B: My / Alex. / name's _____

b. A: sport? / favorite / What's / your _____
   B: Basketball.

c. A: What's your favorite place?
   B: Paris. / My / place / favorite / is _____

d. A: favorite / Who's / sportsperson? / your _____
   B: Serene Williams.

e. A: What's your favorite team?
   B: team / New / Knicks. / My / York / favorite / is / the _____

f. A: What's John's favorite sport?
   B: John's / is / favorite / tennis / sport _____

3 **Complete the chat.**

Workbook Unit 2

4 Look at the table and mark the sentences *T* (true) or *F* (false).

	Mon	Tue	Wed	Thu	Fri	Sat	Sun
Morning	Singing	Judo	Art	Judo	Art	Cycling	Cycling
Afternoon	Yoga	Photography	Yoga	Photography	Yoga	Judo	Judo
Evening	Ceramics	Swimming	Ceramics	Swimming	Dance	Swimming	Yoga

a. Singing is on Monday mornings. ____

b. Photography is on Tuesday and Friday evenings. ____

c. It is possible to do yoga on Tuesdays. ____

d. It is possible to go swimming on Tuesday, Thursday, and Saturday evenings. ____

e. There are dance classes on the weekend. ____

f. There are no ceramics classes Monday to Friday. ____

5 Underline the correct option to complete the exchanges.

a. A: Are you on the soccer team?

B: Yes, *I am/I'm.*

b. A: How old are you?

B: *I am/I'm not* 16.

c. A: Where *are/is* you from?

B: *I'm/I'm not* from New Mexico.

d. A: *Are/Is* you Canadian?

B: No, *I'm not/I am.* I'm French.

e. A: *Are/Is* you at Granville Academy?

B: Yes, *I am/I'm.*

6 Use the prompts to write sentences.

a. My favorite singer / Lorde. She / New Zealand. She / great!

_____

b. My favorite rock band / U2. The singer / Bono. He / Dublin.

_____

c. My favorite pop star / Katy Perry. She / the US. She / very popular.

_____

d. My favorite R&B artist / Bruno Mars. He / singer-songwriter. He / producer too.

_____

Workbook Unit 2

7 Unscramble the words to form sentences.

a. Alison? / you / Are

_____

b. Rebecca. / am / No, / I

_____

c. English / Are / teacher? / you / the

_____

d. Yes, / correct. / that's

_____

e. is / Hi, / my / Alex. / name

_____

f. Nice / Alex. / meet / to / you. / Hi,

_____

8 Write an e-mail to register for a club or activity. Include the following information.

- Your name
- Where you are a student
- Your favorite subject(s) at school
- Two classes you want to register for

9 Complete the conversation with information about Jenna.

RECEPTIONIST: Welcome to Madison Community Center.

JENNA: Thank you! I want to join, please.

RECEPTIONIST: Great! What's 1) _____ name?

JENNA: 2) _____ Jenna Sharp.

RECEPTIONIST: Nice to meet you Jenna! How old are you?

JENNA: 3) _____.

RECEPTIONIST: 4) _____ you a student?

JENNA: 5) _____.

RECEPTIONIST: Are you a student at Madison High?

JENNA: 6) _____. I'm a student at Granville Academy.

RECEPTIONIST: Great! And what is 7) _____ phone number?

JENNA: 8) _____ phone number is (602) 208-2099.

RECEPTIONIST: OK! Wait a minute while I print your membership card.

JENNA: Thanks!

Madison Community Center

NAME: Jenna Sharp
AGE: 15
OCCUPATION: Student
SCHOOL: Granville Academy

118 Unit 2

⌄ Self-Assessment
Unit 2

Think about Unit 2. Write your impressions about each section of the unit.
Include what you learned and how you improved.

Unit Opener

My World

Views

Out and About

⌄ What do I have to do to learn more?

◯ Pay more attention in class.

◯ Do more practice exercises.

◯ Participate more in class.

◯ Study more at home.

◯ Read and listen to English in my free time.

◯ Practice writing and speaking.

◯ Other: _____

Unit 2 119

Workbook Unit 3

1 Complete each sentence.

a. Andy is from the _____. He is British.

b. Serena is from the USA. She's _____.

c. Ayrton is from _____. He's Brazilian.

d. Gustavo is from Mexico. He's _____.

e. Yvonne is from France. She's _____.

f. Carla is from _____. She's Spanish.

2 Unscramble the words to form sentences.

a. Adele / Where / from? / is

_____

b. She's / the / UK. / from

_____

c. Liam / American? / is / Hemsworth

_____

d. No, / He / he / is / Australia. / isn't. / from

_____

e. from? / Where / he / is

_____

f. India / He's / from

_____

g. from / Is / Brazil? / she

_____

h. Spain. / she / from / No, / She / is / isn't.

_____

3 Use the prompts to write the conversation from the game show.

HOST: OK, next celebrity… Natalie Portman.

1) _____ (where / from?)

PATTY: 2) _____ (is / England?)

HOST: No. Maria, what do you think?

MARIA: 3) _____ (she / French / ?)

HOST: No, she isn't. Patty, do you want to answer again?

PATTY: 4) _____ (not / British) and

5) _____ (not / French) Oh…

6) _____ (she / Israel / ?)

HOST: Yes, you're right!

Workbook Unit 3

4 Unscramble the words to form questions and answers.

a. is / Mexican / What / flag? / color / the

_____

white, / and / green, / It / is / red.

_____

b. Canyon? / the / Where / Grand / is

_____

It / in / the / is / USA.

_____

c. Timberlake? / Who / Justin / is

_____

singer. / a / He / famous / is

_____

d. How / spell / you / red? / do

_____

R-E-D. / is / It

_____

5 Write the question words to complete the exchanges.

a. _____ is the White House?

It's in Washington, D.C.

b. _____ is the British flag?

It is red, white, and blue.

c. _____ is the leader of the rock band U2?

His name is Bono.

d. _____ do you spell Jamaica?

J-A-M-A-I-C-A.

e. _____ is the capital of Argentina?

Buenos Aires.

6 Underline the correct words.

a. Are _you/he_ from Spain?

No, we're from Portugal.

b. Are your clothes traditional?

Yes, _they're/they aren't_ special flamenco costumes.

c. _You are/Are you_ singers or dancers?

Are we/We're dancers only.

Unit 3   121

Workbook Unit 3

7 Complete the dialogue with the correct form of the verb *to be.*

A: 1) _____ you a pop group?

B: No, we 2) _____ . We 3) _____
a rock band.

A: 4) _____ the guitarist in the group?

B: No, I'm not. The guitarist 5) _____ Tracy.

A: Where 6) _____ you from?

B: 7) _____ from California.

A: How many players 8) _____ in
your group?

B: Four.

A: 9) _____ you all American?

B: No, we 10) _____ . The drummer and
the guitarist 11) _____ Canadian.

8 Read the information. Write a paragraph about the group.

Name of the group:	The Wave Searchers
Country/City:	Sydney, Australia
Type of music:	Rock music
Group members:	Ashley Fallon – guitarist Troy James – bass player Matt Fitzpatrick – singer Allison Bennett – drummer

_____

_____

_____

_____

_____

_____

_____

_____

⌄ Self-Assessment   Unit 3

Think about Unit 3. Write your impressions about each section of the unit.
Include what you learned and how you improved.

Unit Opener

My World

Views

Out and About

⌄ What do I have to do to learn more?

◯ Pay more attention in class.   ◯ Do more practice exercises.

◯ Participate more in class.   ◯ Study more at home.

◯ Read and listen to English in my free time.   ◯ Practice writing and speaking.

◯ Other: _____

Unit 3 123

Workbook Unit 4

1 Complete the crossword.

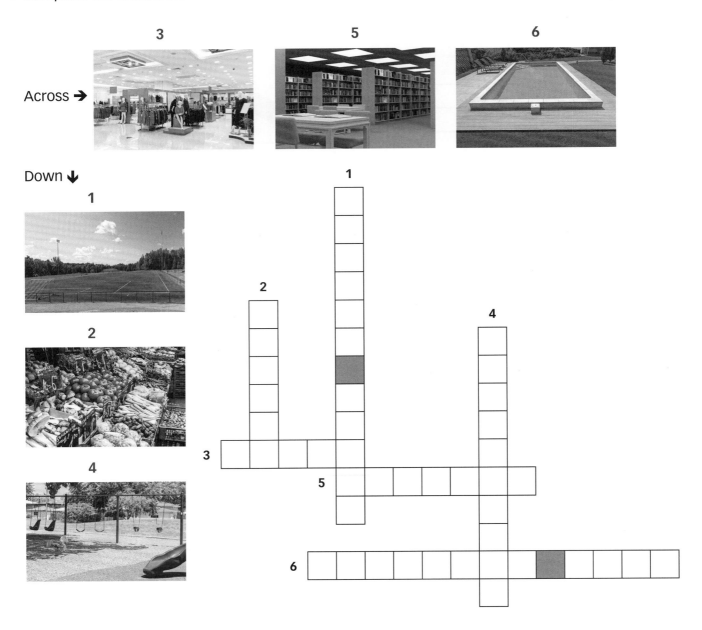

2 Complete the dialogue with the correct words from the box.

Is there   there isn't   there aren't   Are there   there are

A: 1) _____ a library in your town?
B: Yes, there is one library.
A: Is there a swimming pool?
B: No, 2) _____ a swimming pool.
A: Are there museums?
B: No, 3) _____ any.
A: 4) _____ parks?
B: Yes, there are two parks.

A: Is there a supermarket?
B: There is a market but 5) _____ a supermarket.
A: 6) _____ any Mexican restaurants?
B: Yes, 7) _____ three.
A: 8) _____ a music store?
B: Yes, there is one.

124   Unit 4

Workbook Unit 4

3 Use the information to write sentences with *there is* and *there are*.

a. _____

(two sports fields/near my home)

b. _____

(a swimming pool/in the school?)

c. _____

(not/swimming pool/school)

d. _____

(a big library/near the school)

e. _____

(restaurants?)

f. _____

(two restaurants)

g. _____

(not/many parks/near my home)

4 Complete the paragraph with the correct articles.

After you look at our animals, you can relax in

1) _____ Adventurers' Café near 2) _____ Koala

Area. Here you can have 3) _____ quick snack or order

4) _____ delicious meal from our menu. Next to the Café is

our gift shop –5) _____ great place to buy 6) _____

original souvenirs for all your friends.

5 Complete the sentences with *a, an, the,* or — (no article).

a. Sydney is _____ fun city for children.

b. There is _____ aquarium near Harbour Bridge.

c. The Australian Museum has _____ permanent dinosaur collection.

d. Hire a bike in Centennial Park and explore _____ cycle paths.

e. If you like shopping, there are _____ modern shopping malls and markets.

f. _____ shopping mall near our hotel is very big.

g. We are going to see _____ show at the Opera House tonight.

h. Sydney is Australia's _____ largest and most famous city.

Workbook Unit 4

6 Read the clues and solve the crossword puzzle.

Across ➜

2 a rubber suit to swim in cold waters

3 riding ocean waves on a special board

6 spaces to change your clothes in a public place

Down ↓

1 swimming underwater using an air tank

4 a long, light, narrow board used for surfing

5 an object to spray water on a person

7 Read and complete the ad with words from activity 6.

Free Lessons in Let's Go Surfing!

Come and take a free 1) _____ lesson.* Don't worry, you just need to be on time. You can use our air tanks and wear one of our 2) _____.

Or try our specialty: 3) _____ lessons! Bring your own 4) _____ or hire it here.

Come and meet us! We have the best facilities in Bondi Beach. Change your clothes in our spacious 5) _____ and experience our new 6) _____. They feel like rain!

*Valid in summer only!

126   Unit 4

❯ Self-Assessment — Unit 4

Think about Unit 4. Write your impressions about each section of the unit.
Include what you learned and how you improved.

Unit Opener

My World

Views

Out and About

❯ What do I have to do to learn more?

- ☐ Pay more attention in class.
- ☐ Participate more in class.
- ☐ Read and listen to English in my free time.
- ☐ Do more practice exercises.
- ☐ Study more at home.
- ☐ Practice writing and speaking.
- ☐ Other: _____

Workbook Unit 5

1 Circle the correct answer.

   a. Peter is Susan's brother. Susan is Peter's *aunt/cousin/sister*.

   b. Monica is Bill's sister. Bill is Monica's *grandfather/brother/father*.

   c. Elena is Jack's mother. Jack is Elena's *son/brother/father*.

   d. Pedro is my uncle's son. Pedro is my *brother/aunt/cousin*.

   e. Steven is my father's brother. Steven is my *grandfather/uncle/cousin*.

   f. Gloria is my mother's sister. Gloria is my *grandmother/aunt/sister*.

2 Read the text and label the family tree.

   Jackie   Jason   Jaime   Pilar   Clara   David

   My name's Alicia. My father's name is Jaime and my mother's name is Pilar. I have a brother and a sister. Their names are Clara and David. My grandmother's name is Jackie and my grandfather's name is Jason.

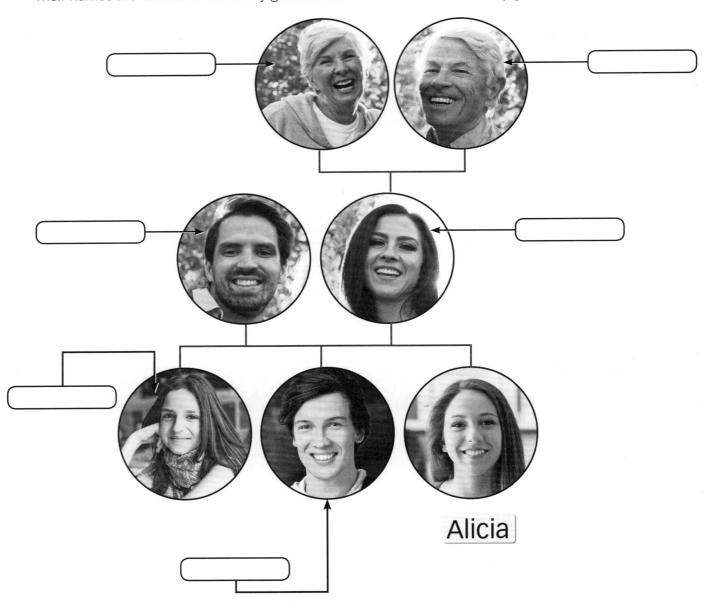

Workbook Unit 5

3 Choose the correct answer.

  a. My wife and I live alone. We *don't/doesn't* have any sons or daughters.
  b. I am allergic. I *doesn't/don't* have any pets.
  c. My aunt loves animals. She *have/has* a dog and a cat.
  d. He buys a lot of food in the supermarket. He *have/has* a big fridge.
  e. She is a student. She *doesn't/don't* have a job.
  f. They are a large family, so they *has/have* a big house.
  g. They cycle to work. They *don't/doesn't* have a car.
  h. I'm an only child. I *haven't/don't have* any brothers or sisters.

4 Complete the sentences with *have, has, don't,* or *doesn't*.

  a. I _____ have a dog but I have a cat.
  b. René _____ have any brothers and sisters.
  c. The Smiths _____ three children.
  d. My father _____ a twin sister. She lives in Japan.
  e. We don't _____ any pets.
  f. Erin _____ an electric guitar. She plays in the garage.

5 Complete the dialogue with *this, that, these,* or *those*.

Lys: What's 1) _____?
Charly: 2) _____ is my new guitar. It's a present from my mom and dad.
Lys: Nice jeans! Are 3) _____ from your parents too?
Charly: No, 4) _____ are from my sister.

Workbook Unit 5

6 Complete the text with the correct answers.

> nose   hair   eyes   face   mouth   ears

Mark is my little brother. He is a very tall baby. He has a round 1) _____ with a big 2) _____ with no teeth, and big 3) _____. He has short 4) _____ and bright 5) _____. He has a small 6) _____.

7 Underline the correct answer.

a. Peter is *Susan/Susan's/Susans* brother.
b. Mr. Avon is *Matt/Matt's/Matts'* uncle.
c. The boy plays with his *sister's/sister/sisters'* guitar.
d. The teacher takes the *student's/student/students* homework.
e. My *family's/families'/familys* last name is Cason.
f. My *mother's/mothers/mothers'* name is Lucy.

8 Write sentences with the information in parentheses.

a. (Jason / short / hair)
_____

b. (my friends / smartphones / new)
_____

c. (my father / big / ears)
_____

d. (my best friend / birthday / Friday)
_____

e. (he / play / brother / toys)
_____

f. (my grandparents / house / small)
_____

Self-Assessment Unit 5

Think about Unit 5. Write your impressions about each section of the unit. Include what you learned and how you improved.

Unit Opener

My World

Views

Out and About

What do I have to do to learn more?

◯ Pay more attention in class.

◯ Do more practice exercises.

◯ Participate more in class.

◯ Study more at home.

◯ Read and listen to English in my free time.

◯ Practice writing and speaking.

◯ Other: _____

Unit 5 131

Workbook Unit 6

1 Complete the questions and answers on Simon's page.

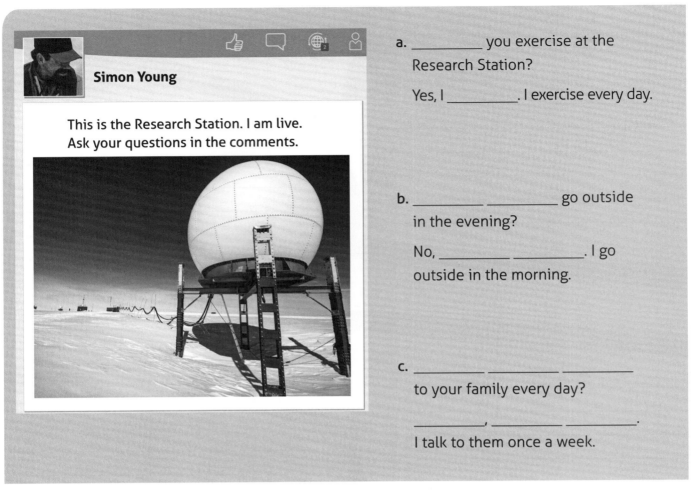

a. _____ you exercise at the Research Station?
Yes, I _____. I exercise every day.

b. _____ _____ go outside in the evening?
No, _____ _____. I go outside in the morning.

c. _____ _____ _____ to your family every day?
_____, _____ _____. I talk to them once a week.

2 Complete the sentences with the correct word from the box.

| do   get   take   breakfast   talk   exercise |

a. I _____ up at 7:00 a.m.
b. I always eat _____ before I go to school.
c. I _____ to my family before I go to bed.
d. I _____ a shower in the morning.
e. I don't _____ in a gym.
f. I _____ my homework in the evening.

3 Complete the sentences with the correct form of the verbs.

a. I _____ coffee for breakfast. (not drink)
b. You _____ breakfast at home. (eat)
c. You _____ a shower in the evening. (not take)
d. I _____ a uniform. (not wear)
e. You _____ to music in bed. (not listen)
f. I _____ TV in my bedroom. (not watch)
g. You _____ your homework in the evening. (do)

132   Unit 6

Workbook Unit 6

4 Unscramble the sentences.

a. TV / dinner? / Do / watch / you / after

_____

b. I / No, / don't.

_____

c. read / in / you / bed? / Do

_____

d. do. / I / Yes,

_____

e. exercise / Do / in / morning? / the / you

_____

f. I / every / I / exercise / Yes, / do. / day.

_____

5 Classify the verbs.

> cycle   do   go   like

a. Main verb + s: _____   b. Main verb + es: _____

6 Write questions for Martin Doyle (page 65).

a. (play chess after school)

_____

b. (like sports)

_____

c. (wake up late on Saturday)

_____

d. (watch TV)

_____

e. (walk home)

_____

7 Rewrite the incorrect words.

a. Does Eric ~~listens~~ _____ to music in the evening?

   Yes, he ~~do~~ _____.

b. ~~Do~~ _____ he play the guitar in his free time?

   No, he ~~don't~~ _____. He plays the piano.

c. Does Cindy ~~plays~~ _____ chess at school?

   Yes, she ~~don't~~ _____.

d. ~~Do~~ _____ she like cycling?

   No, she ~~does~~ _____. She likes running on weekends.

Workbook Unit 6

8 Complete the sentences with the correct form of the verbs.

a. Kevin _____ (not watch) TV in the mornings.

b. He _____ (have) lunch in the school cafeteria every day.

c. He _____ (cycle) to school in the mornings.

d. Alicia _____ (take) a shower in the evenings.

e. She _____ (eat) pizza for lunch on Fridays.

f. She _____ (listen) to rap music all the time.

9 Label the clocks with the times.

| five past eight   ten to three   three o'clock   a quarter to nine   a quarter past one   ten thirty |

a. It's _____ .

d. It's _____ .

b. It's _____ .

e. It's _____ .

c. It's _____ .

f. It's _____ .

10 Write questions to interview Dao and Chati (page 68).

a. you / live in a small village?

_____

b. your parents / walk with you in the jungle?

_____

c. you / see wild animals?

_____

d. your friends / go to the same school?

_____

✔ Self-Assessment   Unit 6

Think about Unit 6. Write your impressions about each section of the unit.
Include what you learned and how you improved.

Unit Opener

My World

Views

Out and About

✔ What do I have to do to learn more?

☐ Pay more attention in class.

☐ Do more practice exercises.

☐ Participate more in class.

☐ Study more at home.

☐ Read and listen to English in my free time.

☐ Practice writing and speaking.

☐ Other: _____

Workbook Unit 7

1 Match the words to the images.

bacon   bread   milk   apple   egg   lettuce   cheese   orange juice

a. _____

c. _____

e. _____

b. _____

d. _____

f. _____

2 Match the sandwiches with the sandwich labels. Then invent a brand and create a sandwich label for your own favorite sandwich.

a.

b.

The Sandwich Store
Super fresh!
Ham, cheese and lettuce

Joe's Sandwich Factory
All Local Ingredients:
Egg and Tomato

3 Classify the sentences.

some   any

a. There is _____ chocolate.
b. There are _____ bananas.
c. There isn't _____ bread.
d. Are there _____ bananas?
e. There is _____ bread.
f. There aren't _____ apples.
g. There are _____ grapes.
h. Is there _____ soda?

Workbook Unit 7

4 Write questions for the answers.

a. _____

No, there isn't any soda.

b. _____

Yes, there are some bananas.

c. _____

No, there isn't any bread.

d. _____

Yes, there are some apples.

e. _____

No, there isn't any cheese.

f. _____

Yes, there are some eggs.

g. _____

No, there aren't any tomatoes.

5 Work in pairs. Complete the lists with food items.

In the Refrigerator

Shopping List

> Use the lists to write a dialogue.

Workbook Unit 7

6 Complete the crossword.

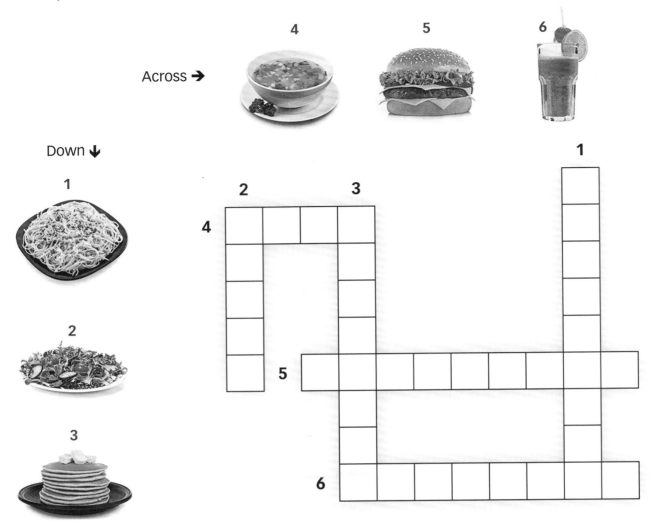

7 Complete the sentences with the correct word.

a. I can't eat my soup. I need a ____spoon____.

b. I need a _____ to cut the orange.

c. Don't take the food with your fingers. Use a _____.

d. You have ketchup on your face. Use your _____ to clean it.

e. Let's ask for a _____. I don't know what to order.

f. Get a _____ and I'll give you some food.

8 Complete the conversation.

WAITER: Hi, 1) _____ you like to order?

DAN: Yes, I'd 2) _____ two hot dogs, please.

WAITER: What 3) _____ some salad?

DAN: No, thanks.

WAITER: What 4) _____ you like to drink?

DAN: 5) _____ like some water, please.

WAITER: Would 6) _____ like anything else?

DAN: No, that's all. Thanks!

✔ Self-Assessment   Unit 7

Think about Unit 7. Write your impressions about each section of the unit.
Include what you learned and how you improved.

Unit Opener

My World

Views

Out and About

✔ What do I have to do to learn more?

☐ Pay more attention in class.   ☐ Do more practice exercises.

☐ Participate more in class.   ☐ Study more at home.

☐ Read and listen to English in my free time. ☐ Practice writing and speaking.

☐ Other: _____

Workbook Unit 8

1 Use the prompts to write the conversations.

Conversation 1

a. VISITOR: what / you / do / ?

_____

b. STUDENT: I / collect / old school books

_____

c. VISITOR: you / throw out / the old books?

_____

d. STUDENT: no / recycle / them

_____

Conversation 2

a. VISITOR: what / you / do / ?

_____

b. STUDENT: I / make / a table

_____

c. VISITOR: you / make / the table from paper?

_____

d. STUDENT: yes

_____

2 Match the columns.

a. Hi Megan. What are you doing? ____ Yes, I always wash them.

b. Are you washing the dishes? ____ I'm studying science.

c. What are you collecting? ____ No, it's an app for editing pictures.

d. Are you making a website? ____ Old books for charity.

3 Use the words to write the dialogues.

a. *Are you collecting paper and plastic?*

   Yes, I'm recycling them.

b. _____ (what / do?)

   _____ (I / create a website)

c. _____ (tidy up your room?)

   _____ (no / make my bed)

d. _____ (what / study)

   _____ (study / math)

Workbook Unit 8

4 Match the columns.

a. dining room   ___ a room where you sleep
b. garage   ___ a place to cook food
c. bedroom   ___ an area where you can have flowers and grass
d. kitchen   ___ a room for eating meals
e. living room   ___ a place to park your car
f. yard   ___ a place to sit, watch TV, and relax

5 Complete the sentences.

a. I sleep very well at night. My new _____ is very comfortable.
b. In America, people don't usually sit on the floor to eat. They sit on a _____.
c. We have a big _____ for watching TV at home. Four people can sit on it.
d. We have a beautiful red _____ on the floor of our living room.
e. While my mom cooks dinner, I set the _____ before we eat.
f. I keep my clothes in a _____ in my room.

6 Underline the correct answers.

Rory is in his garage. He is 1) *repairing/doing/making* his car. Then he sees his robot, RB5. The robot 2) *is standing/is feeling/feels* by the door. It 3) *is looking/standing/making* out into the street.

4) "*What are/What is/Are* you doing, RB5?" Rory asks.

"I 5) *am thinking/is thinking/are thinking*," RB5 answers.

"Can you help me, please?" asks Rory. RB5 turns to Rory. It 6) *is holding/are holding/holding* something in its hand.

7) "*What are/What is/Are you* OK?" asks Rory.

"No, I'm not," says the robot.

Rory sees that smoke 8) *is coming/are coming/is playing* out of the robot's mouth. Then RB5 starts to move towards him.

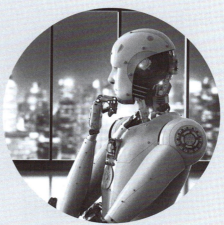

Workbook Unit 8

7 Use the information to write the conversation.

Conversation 1

A: (Dad / where / you)
_____

B: (I / office)
_____

A: (help / buy a book)
_____

B: (sure)
_____

Conversation 2

A: (Ray / set the table, / please)
_____

B: (sorry / I / do / homework)
_____

A: (OK / worry)
_____

8 Classify the sentences.

> Ability   Request

a. Can you fry an egg? _____

b. Can you take out the trash, please? _____

c. I can make an omelet in 25.24 seconds. _____

d. I can toss pancakes. _____

e. Can she make a chocolate sculpture? _____

f. Can you water the plants? _____

✔ Self-Assessment

Unit 8

Think about Unit 8. Write your impressions about each section of the unit. Include what you learned and how you improved.

Unit Opener

My World

Views

Out and About

✔ What do I have to do to learn more?

- ☐ Pay more attention in class.
- ☐ Participate more in class.
- ☐ Read and listen to English in my free time.
- ☐ Do more practice exercises.
- ☐ Study more at home.
- ☐ Practice writing and speaking.
- ☐ Other: _____

Book 1

Publisher
Lauren Robbins

Series Editor
Simon Cupit, Ana Luiza Couto

Editors
Arnoldo Langner Romero, Imelda Vazquez Córdova,
Jorge Mancera Cardós, Mariana Albertini

Authors
Michael Downie, David Gray, Juan Manuel Jimenez

Proofreading
Aaron Burkholder, Angélica Soares

Series Design
Daniela Ibarra

Cover Design
Gilciane Munhoz, João Brito, Carla Almeida Freire

Cover Illustration
Indio San

Design Coordination
Daniela Ibarra

Layout and DTP
Daniela Ibarra, Rocío Echávarri R.

Illustration
Antonio Rocha, David Peón, Diego Omar Uriarte

Photography
© Thinkstock, 2014
© AFP, 2014
© Other Images, 2014
© Only One Direction, 2014
© Shutterstock, 2018
© iStockphoto, 2018
© Getty Images, 2018
http://tahuantinsuyo.org

Production
Ulisses Pires, Juliano de Arruda Fernandes, Ivan Toledo

Picture Research
Josiane Laurentino, Susan Eiko

The trademark University of Dayton Publishing is the property of University of Dayton. Unauthorized copying, reproduction, hiring, and lending prohibited.

U.D. Publishing, S.A. de C.V., is the exclusive licensee of the University of Dayton Publishing brand.

University of Dayton
300 College Park
Dayton, OH 45469

i-World 1
Student's Book & Workbook / Teacher's Book
First edition, 2018
© U.D. Publishing, S.A. de C.V., México.
All rights reserved.
br.educamos.sm

Dados Internacionais de Catalogação na Publicação (CIP)
(Câmara Brasileira do Livro, SP, Brasil)

Downie, Michael
i-world 1 : student's book & workbook / teacher's book
Michael Downie, David Gray, Juan Manuel Jimenez. —
São Paulo : Edições SM, 2018.

Inclui CD.
ISBN 978-85-418-2018-9 (S.B.)
ISBN 978-85-418-2022-6 (T.B.)

1. Inglês (Ensino fundamental) I. Gray, David.
II. Jimenez, Juan Manuel. III. Título.

18-15014   CDD-372.652

Índices para catálogo sistemático:
1. Inglês : Ensino fundamental 372.652

Iolanda Rodrigues Biode - Bibliotecária - CRB-8/10014

All rights reserved. No part of this book may be reproduced, stored in a retrieval system, or transmitted in any form or by any means, electronic, mechanical, photocopying, recording or otherwise, without prior permission in writing of the publishers.

Printed in Brazil/*Impresso no Brasil*

i-World 1
Student's Book & Workbook / Teacher's Book
Printed in April 2018 at Ricargraf

Rua Tenente Lycurgo Lopes da Cruz, 55
Água Branca 05036-120 São Paulo SP Brasil
Tel. 11 2111-7400
edicoessm@grupo-sm.com
www.edicoessm.com.br